which?
essential guides

GI
IN ~~~~~~~~

“ More and more people are being drawn into the inheritance tax net. You have two choices: accept that you'll be leaving money to HMRC or take steps now to reduce that chance. ”

Jonquil Lowe

About the author

Jonquil Lowe is an economist who worked for several years in the City as an investment analyst, and is a former head of the Money Group at the Consumers' Association. She now works as a freelance financial researcher and journalist and holds the Diploma in Financial Planning (formerly called the Advanced Financial Planning Certificate). Jonquil writes extensively on all areas of personal finance and is the author of several other books, including *The Pension Handbook*, *Be Your Own Financial Adviser* and *The Which? Guide to Money in Retirement*, and is co-author of *The FT Guide to Personal Tax*.

GIVING AND INHERITING

JONQUIL LOWE

Which? Books are commissioned and published by Which? Ltd,
2 Marylebone Road, London NW1 4DF
Project management for Which? Books: Luke Block
Email: books@which.co.uk

Distributed by Littlehampton Book Services Ltd, Faraday Close, Durrington, Worthing,
West Sussex BN13 3RB

British Library Cataloguing in Publication Data
A catalogue record for this book is available from the British Library

ISBN 978 1 84490 032 9

Although the author and publishers endeavour to make sure the information
in this book is accurate and up-to-date, it is only a general guide. Before taking action
on financial, legal, or medical matters you should consult a qualified professional adviser,
who can consider your individual circumstances. The author and publishers can not
accordingly accept liability for any loss or damage suffered as a consequence of relying
on the information contained in this guide.

Author's acknowledgements
The author would like to thank Ian Robinson and Teresa Fritz for their helpful suggestions.

Source material
HM Revenue & Customs: p7 (tax facts), p11 (inheritance tax-free limits); Will Aid: p137
(will facts and figures).

Edited by: Emma Callery
Designed by: Bob Vickers
Index by: Lynda Swindells
Cover photographs by: Getty Images Ltd
Printed and bound by Scotprint, Scotland

For a full list of Which? Books, please call 01903 828557, access our website at
www.which.co.uk, or write to Littlehampton Book Services.
For other enquiries call 0800 252 100.

Contents

Introduction

Inheritance tax (IHT) is no longer just a tax on the rich. It can catch ordinary people with modest wealth.

Inheritance tax used to be a tax on the people who lived in stately homes, drove Rolls-Royces and relaxed on yachts in St-Tropez. Now it is a concern for average families with semis in suburbia.

Jargon buster

Asset A handy shorthand word for something that you own. It could be cash, investments, a house, your personal possessions, or anything else. Something you owe to someone else - such as an outstanding mortgage loan - is called a 'liability'

Estate Everything you own at the time you die less everything you owe. For example, your estate includes your home, your furniture, car, personal possessions, savings and investments less your mortgage, tax you owe, unpaid bills, and so on. If you own something jointly with someone else (or have a joint mortgage or other debts), your estate includes just your share

Inheritance tax (IHT) A tax on many gifts you make in your lifetime and on your death if they exceed a tax-free limit

Lifetime gifts A gift you make while you are still alive rather than on your death

This shift in the scope of IHT has not come about through any dramatic change in the law. As house prices have risen, especially in the south of England, more and more ordinary people are being quietly drawn into the IHT net.

Inheritance tax applies to some **lifetime gifts** but is mainly a tax on the **estate** you leave when you die. Everyone can pass on a certain amount tax-free, but the tax-free threshold has risen in most years only in line with general price inflation. The price of houses – which make up a large part of most ordinary people's wealth – has risen much faster and so, increasingly, more estates are spilling over the tax-free limit. IHT then takes a big, 40 per cent bite out of the excess.

Some view the expansion of IHT as unfair. It's argued that people have already paid taxes on the earnings used to buy their homes and so paying IHT amounts to a double tax bill. Others say the massive rise in house prices over recent years is a windfall and, if IHT were abolished, governments would simply need to raise money through other, even more unpopular, taxes.

 To check the current inheritance tax-free allowance and rates, see page 52 or the HM Revenue & Customs website at www.hmrc.gov.uk/rates/inheritance.htm.

6

SHOULD YOU BE WORRIED?

Most people do not pay IHT during their lifetime. IHT on your death is a tax bill for your heirs not you. So you do not need to worry about finding the money yourself to pay an IHT bill. But you might be worried about IHT if:

- **You want to leave an inheritance.** Many people like to know that, after they are gone, they are still able to help their family and friends, especially their children, by leaving them money or other **assets**. IHT can take a big chunk out of what you leave.
- **Someone could face financial hardship when you die.** Anything you leave to your husband, wife or civil partner is normally exempt from IHT. But this exemption does not extend to an unmarried partner or other people who may depend on you financially. For example, an unmarried partner, sister, brother, daughter or son who lives with you might have to sell the home you have shared in order to pay a tax bill on your death.
- **You want to set up trusts in your lifetime.** Following changes in the 2006 Budget, most types of trust may now trigger IHT bills in your lifetime. Trusts are not just for people with complicated affairs and a lot of wealth. They are useful, for example, where you want to make gifts to children but want to avoid them squandering the money in the exuberance of youth.

- **You don't like the idea of giving your wealth to the taxman!** Most of us feel we have struggled to accumulate a little bit of financial security and don't want to see it going into the coffers of HM Revenue & Customs.

Tax facts

In 2007-8, IHT is expected to raise £4 billion and was paid by six out of 100 estates. This is double the number of estates paying the tax ten years ago.

❝A partner, sister, brother, daughter or son who lives with you might have to sell the home you have shared in order to pay a tax bill on your death.❞

Inheritance tax on death

If your estate exceeds the tax-free threshold, inheritance tax takes a bite out of the excess.

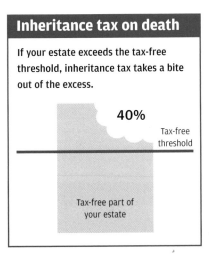

40%

Tax-free threshold

Tax-free part of your estate

7

WHAT CAN YOU DO?

IHT used to be called a voluntary tax because there were so many ways to avoid paying it. That is no longer true, especially if most of your wealth is tied up in your home. To reduce or eliminate a tax bill on your wealth, you have three broad options: spend it, give it away or insure against the tax. But there are many ways to put these options into effect. They include:

- Making full use of your tax-free allowance, especially if you are a couple.
- Writing a will and keeping it up to date.
- Thinking about how you share your home and other assets with other people and choosing the most tax-efficient ways to do this.
- Making full use of the opportunities to make tax-free gifts during your lifetime.
- Understanding what tax-free gifts you can make in your will.
- Considering unlocking some of your wealth now to spend and enjoy in your lifetime.
- Looking at trusts as a way of ensuring gifts are used in the way you intend and using trusts tax efficiently.
- Using insurance policies both as a way of making gifts and for ensuring that any tax can be paid.

Chapters 1–6 of this guide consider your options for making lifetime gifts. Chapters 7–10 look at tax at the time of death and what steps you can take in your lifetime to minimise its impact on your heirs. The final chapter looks at what your heirs themselves can do to inherit tax efficiently.

With the *Which? Essential Guide* to *Giving and Inheriting* at your side, you can cross HM Revenue & Customs off your list of beneficiaries or at least relegate them to the bottom.

This edition of the *Which? Essential Guide* to *Giving and Inheriting* is up to date as at March 2007 and includes changes announced in that year's budget.

❝ You have three broad options: spend it, give it away or insure against the tax. ❞

If you are writing your own will, sorting out someone else's will, setting up a trust, considering tax avoidance schemes, or your situation is at all complex or involves large sums of money, please note that it is important to consult a legal and/or tax adviser. See Contacts on page 212.

8

Lifetime gift planning

Making gifts during your lifetime is the main way to reduce an inheritance tax bill on your estate when you die, though you need to steer a course around other taxes that can hit lifetime gifts. Top priority is making sure you do not jeopardise your financial security by giving away more than you can afford. Giving something away now but retaining the right to use it during your lifetime might seem the answer, but the tax authorities have thought of that one too.

1

Tax and lifetime gifts

A key way to avoid or reduce tax at your death is to give away your wealth during your lifetime. But you need to watch out for possible tax on your lifetime gifts.

Inheritance taxes have been with us for a long time, but the rules tend to vary with the political party in power. Typically, Conservative governments take a more lenient approach towards taxing wealth than Labour administrations. When the Labour government came to power in 1997, it inherited a fairly loose IHT regime. The focus was on taxing wealth as it changed hands on death but most lifetime gifts were either completely tax-free or tax-free if the giver survived seven years. In 2006, the present government tightened up the regime considerably by making most lifetime gifts, other than outright gifts to individuals, taxable. Some experts speculate that, in future, the rules might change again to bring even more lifetime gifts into the tax net. They could be wrong but, in this uncertain climate, it may be better to sort out any lifetime giving sooner rather than later.

In addition to IHT, you need to consider the impact of capital gains tax (CGT).

In this uncertain climate, it may be better to sort out any lifetime giving sooner rather than later.

WHY MAKE LIFETIME GIFTS?

There are many reasons for making gifts – to help your children as they set out into adult life, to help other family members or friends and to support a charity are a few examples. Another reason is to reduce a potential IHT bill at your death.

IHT is charged on a rolling total of gifts you make over the last seven years. When you die, the estate you leave is treated as your final gift. Whether or not tax is due on your estate depends on whether the value of your estate plus other gifts you have made in the last seven years exceeds the IHT-free threshold.

To check out in detail changes the government made in 2006 to inheritance tax on lifetime gifts, see the HM Treasury website at www.hm-treasury.gov.uk/budget/budget_06/bud_bud06_index.cfm.

10

Working out inheritance tax on your estate

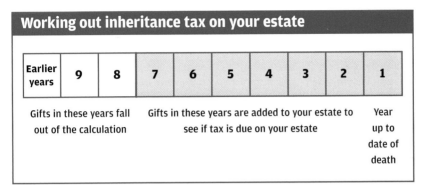

Earlier years	9	8	7	6	5	4	3	2	1

Gifts in these years fall out of the calculation

Gifts in these years are added to your estate to see if tax is due on your estate

Year up to date of death

Gifts you made more than seven years before death drop out of the calculation. It therefore follows that, provided you survive for seven years, any gifts you make now will reduce the value of your estate and so could save tax on the estate.

Some gifts are tax-free – such as gifts on marriage and up to £3,000 a year of gifts to anyone (see pages 13–14) – and don't come into the calculation. You can make these at any time and, regardless of how long you survive, they reduce the value of your estate.

Inheritance tax-free limit

Tax year	Tax-free limit
2007-8	£300,000
2008-9	£312,000
2009-10	£325,000
2010-11	£350,000

Do not give away in your lifetime money or assets that you can't afford or might need later on.

HOW LIFETIME GIFTS MAY BE TAXED

You need to be aware of two main taxes when making lifetime gifts: inheritance tax (IHT) and capital gains tax (CGT). Some gifts affect your income tax position too.

Inheritance tax and lifetime gifts

For IHT purposes, there are three types of lifetime gift:

- **Tax-free gifts** (also called 'exempt transfers'). There is no IHT on these.

For a complete list of the current inheritance tax-free allowance and rates, see page 52.

11

- **Taxable gifts** (also called 'chargeable transfers'). Most gifts to **trusts** are taxable gifts. The gift is added to any other taxable gifts you have made during the last seven years. If the total comes to more than the tax-free threshold in force at the time of your latest gift, IHT at the lifetime rate of 20 per cent is due on the gift at the time it is made.
- **Potentially exempt transfers (PETs)**. Gifts direct from one person to another count as PETs. A PET is tax-free provided you survive for seven years after making it. If you die within seven years, the PET is reclassified as a taxable gift.

CGT and lifetime gifts

CGT is a tax on the increase in value of something during the time that you have owned it. If you sell the thing at a profit, CGT is a tax on that profit. When you give something away, tax can be due on the potential profit you could have made.

Some things are always free of CGT, such as gifts of cash. Some types of transaction are CGT-free, such as gifts to charity. Even when something is taxable, there are various reliefs that reduce or even eliminate the tax bill. One of the most important is the yearly CGT allowance that everyone has. In 2007–8, the allowance is £9,200.

Income tax and lifetime gifts

In some situations, you can be taxed on income from something you have given away. This applies, for example, to gifts you have made to a trust if you can benefit from the trust and gifts you make to your dependent child if the income earned by the gift exceeds £100 a year.

In other situations, the government encourages you to make gifts through tax incentives for you and/or the recipient. This applies to gifts to charities and certain gifts to children.

MINIMISE INHERITANCE TAX ON LIFETIME GIFTS

The following points are a round-up of straightforward ways to save IHT on lifetime gifts.

Jargon buster

Trust A legal arrangement where one or more people (the trustees) hold money or assets (the trust property) to be used for the benefit of one or more other people (the beneficiaries). The trust's rules can set conditions on how the trust property is held and used

For details of tax-free gifts, see Chapter 2. You can find out more about taxable gifts and PETs in Chapter 3.

Make tax-free gifts

For a full list of tax-free gifts see Chapter 2. Here are three of the best:

- **Gifts that are normal expenditure out of income.** If you establish a regular pattern of giving that you can manage out of your income without reducing your living standards, the gifts are IHT free. The beauty of this exemption is that it can apply to gifts of any amount. It could cover, for example, monthly or yearly premiums you pay for a life insurance policy that, on your death, will pay out direct to the person you have chosen. It can also cover irregular payments made according to a regular pattern – for example, giving each of your children a set sum on their 18th birthdays.
- **Gifts to your husband, wife or civil partner.** Each of you has your own IHT, capital gains tax and income tax allowances. If one of you holds most of the family assets, the other person could be wasting their allowances. To ensure those allowances are used to the full, consider spreading your assets more evenly between you (sometimes called 'equalising your estates'). Because gifts between husbands, wives and civil partners are normally tax-free, you can achieve this spreading without triggering a tax bill.

If your husband, wife or civil partner is domiciled (i.e. has their permanent home) abroad, tax-free gifts to them are limited to £55,000.

Your gifts must be genuine, so you need to be confident that your relationship is sound.

- **Yearly tax-free allowance.** Each year you can make tax-free gifts up to £3,000 that are not covered by any of the other IHT exemptions. If you don't use up the full allowance one year, you can carry the unused part forward to the next year (but no further), giving you a maximum tax-free allowance of £6,000 for that year.

Use your tax-free limit

Any gifts you make that are not tax-free still will not trigger a tax bill provided your rolling total of gifts over the last seven years does not exceed the tax-free limit.

MINIMISE CAPITAL GAINS TAX ON LIFETIME GIFTS

Here are some straightforward ways to save CGT on lifetime gifts.

For more information about CGT on lifetime gifts, see Chapter 3. Chapter 4 includes information about gifts to trusts. See Chapter 5 for guidance on making gifts to children and Chapter 6 for gifts to charity.

13

Case Study Sara

In May 2007, Sara pays £50,000 into a trust fund to help her three children get through university. She has not made any other gifts in the last seven years. £6,000 of her gift to the trust is covered by this year's tax-free allowance plus her unused tax-free allowance carried from last year. That leaves £44,000 of the gift, but there is no tax on this because it falls comfortably within her tax-free threshold of £300,000.

Make tax-free gifts

For a full list of tax-free gifts see Chapter 2. Here are three of the best:

- Give cash rather than assets. There is no CGT on gifts of cash.
- Give 'chattels' worth £6,000 or less. Where you have a choice, consider giving away a painting, antique furniture or other collectibles rather than, say shares. Provided they are worth £6,000 or less, possessions like these are exempt from CGT.
- Use your tax-free allowance. Everyone can make a certain amount of gains tax-free each year. In 2007–8, the allowance is £9,200.

Make gifts to your wife, husband or civil partner

Each of you has your own IHT, capital gains tax and income tax allowances. If one of you holds most of the family assets, the other person could be wasting their allowances. To ensure those allowances are used to the full, consider spreading your assets more evenly between you.

For CGT purposes, gifts between husbands, wives and civil partners are made on a no-gain-no-loss basis. This means there is no tax bill at the time of the gift. Instead the recipient takes over any gain that had built up and there could be tax on it when they eventually sell or give away the asset. Your gifts must be genuine, so you need to be confident that your relationship is sound.

Case Study Ravi

In 2007–8, Ravi plans to sell some shares. But the shares will realise a taxable profit of £18,400. Although Ravi can set his yearly CGT allowance against the profit, that will still leave £9,200 of gain to be taxed.

Ravi decides to give half his shares to his wife, Mira. There is no tax on the gift because Ravi effectively gives Mira the potential tax bill along with the shares. Mira decides to sell the shares. There is no tax for her to pay because the whole gain is covered by her yearly CGT allowance.

Ravi sells his remaining shares and again there is no tax to pay because his yearly CGT allowance eliminates the whole of his gain.

It is important that Mira was free to use the shares (and the sale proceeds) in any way she liked. The gift would not have been genuine if Ravi had made it only on condition that she used the shares in a particular way.

Lifetime gift planning pitfalls

To save tax, a gift must be genuine. If it's genuine, then you can't get it back later if your circumstances change. So think carefully before making lifetime gifts.

GIVING AWAY MONEY YOU NEED LATER ON

To save IHT, any gifts you make must be genuine. This means you completely give up the thing you give away. Check your current and future financial situation carefully to make sure you can really afford the gift. Be realistic about the future, for example:

- **Losing a partner.** If you are a couple, consider how your financial circumstances might change if you lost your partner through death or divorce.
- **Needing long-term care.** Think what resources you would have if later on you needed help with personal care either in your own home or in a residential home.
- **Inheritance.** Be wary of anticipating money or assets you expect to inherit from someone else. You might not be left the bequest after all or it might be worth less than you had expected.

- **Investment returns.** Use modest assumptions about how your savings and investments might grow in the future and the income they might generate for you.

GIFTS THAT DON'T COUNT FOR INHERITANCE TAX

Especially if most of your wealth is tied up in your home, you might not have much spare cash or other wealth to give away. In that situation, you might be tempted to give something away now but on condition that you carry on using it while you are still alive.

Gifts like this are called 'gifts with reservation' and, for IHT purposes, they continue to count as part of your estate and so do not save any tax at your death. Schemes that get around the gift-with-reservation rules are usually caught instead by the pre-owned assets tax (POAT), which could land you with a tax bill every year based on the value of the benefit you are assumed to get from the asset.

 You can find information about gifts with reservation, the pre-owned assets tax and the limited situations when they don't apply in Chapters 4 and 10.

15

TAX AVOIDANCE AND COMPLICATED TAX PLANNING

Not so long ago, the accepted view was: tax avoidance is legal, tax evasion is not. Tax avoidance was simply the clever but perfectly legal use of quirks in the law to save tax. But HMRC's attitude towards tax avoidance has become increasingly hardened over the years. Although exploiting loopholes in the legislation is not illegal as such, it is deemed to be unfair and a constant stream of new anti-avoidance legislation aims to close down complicated tax-planning schemes as fast as they appear. Therefore, you should approach any such scheme with caution.

If you are attracted to complicated tax planning, always get professional advice and bear in mind the following points:

- **Evasion**. Avoidance may be frowned upon but is not a crime. By contrast, breaking the tax rules is illegal tax evasion for which there are heavy penalties, including the possibility of a prison term.
- **Shams**. The courts are wise to attempts to dress up illegal tax arrangements to look like legal ones.
- **Associated operations**. Even where an arrangement seems to be within the law it may fall foul of the 'associated operations' rules. These have built up through case law and mean that a series of transactions can be looked at as a whole. If they do not have a bona fide commercial motive and have been devised primarily as a way of

saving tax, they can be deemed to be artificial and the tax-saving effects nullified.

- **Revenue challenge**. HMRC is prepared to challenge schemes through the Revenue Commissioners (due to be replaced with a new tribunal system) and subsequently the courts, so there is no guarantee that a complicated scheme that you thought would save tax actually will do so at the end of the day. In addition, you may run the risk of becoming involved in lengthy and costly legal disputes.
- **Changes in the law**. Even if the taxpayer wins a case against HMRC, the government can change the law to close loopholes and ban schemes. Although such changes might not to be retrospective in the strict sense of the word, HMRC moved the goal posts when it introduced the pre-owned assets tax (see Chapter 4) and has made it clear that it is prepared to introduce further 'retroactive' measures if necessary. A retroactive change does not impose a tax bill for past tax years but does impose a tax bill now on actions you took in the past. So any action you take now which seems to save tax could give rise to a future tax bill if the law is changed.

❝HMRC's attitude towards tax avoidance has become increasingly hardened over the years. ❞

16

Tax-free gifts

There are two key taxes to watch out for when you make a lifetime gift: IHT and capital gains tax. This chapter looks at gifts you can make during your lifetime that are free of capital gains tax, free of IHT or free of both.

2

Capital gains tax

If something you own has increased in value up to the time you give it away, normally there would be capital gains tax (CGT) to pay. But some gains are tax-free.

When you give someone something that you own, you are treated for tax purposes as making a 'disposal' of an asset and the tax position is essentially the same as if you had sold it. This means that, if the asset's value at the time you give it away is greater than its value at the time you first started to own it, there could be a CGT bill. But don't panic. Often, you will not have to pay any CGT, because:

- Some assets are outside the scope of CGT.
- Gains from some transactions are always tax-free.

Jargon buster

Asset A handy shorthand word for something that you own. It could be cash, investments, a house, your personal possessions, or anything else

Disposal Usually this means receiving a capital sum from an asset, for example, when you sell it or you receive an insurance pay-out because the asset has been lost or destroyed. But gifts also count as disposals for CGT purposes and you are treated as if you had received the market value of the asset

CGT-free assets and transactions at a glance

The following gifts are either tax-free or there is no tax at the time the gift is made. Conditions may apply and are explained in this chapter.

- Money
- Chattels with a life of no more than 50 years
- Chattels worth £6,000 or less
- Motor vehicles
- Your only or main home
- Some National Savings & Investments products
- Individual savings accounts (ISAs)
- Personal equity plans (PEPs)

- Enterprise Investment Scheme shares
- Venture Capital Trust shares
- Right to receive certain payments
- Gifts between husband and wife or civil partners
- Gifts to charities and some similar bodies
- Gifts of national heritage property
- Gifts if you move abroad for at least five years
- Gifts on death

18

THE SCOPE OF CAPITAL GAINS TAX

CGT is a tax on the disposal of assets. Assets cover virtually all types of possessions: land, buildings (including your home), stocks and shares, paintings, furniture, patents and copyrights, debts owed to you. But some assets are specifically free from CGT.

Money

Assets, for CGT purposes, do not include sterling currency – so a gift of money cannot result in a CGT bill.

Coin collections would not normally count as money. But, by an interesting quirk of the law, sovereigns minted after 1837 do still count as sterling currency and are therefore outside the CGT net. (Sovereigns minted before then and other collectible coins count as 'chattels' – see below.)

There is no CGT on gains from buying and selling foreign money that you have obtained for your own use – for a holiday abroad, say, for buying or running a holiday home abroad or for use during a business trip.

Chattels

This means 'tangible, movable property' – basically your personal belongings, such as clothes, books, compact discs and your household goods, as well as things such as jewellery, antiques, paintings and many other collectibles. An item in this category is exempt from CGT provided:

- It has a predicted useful life of 50 years or less and you have not used it in a business.

Planning point

The special rules for taxing chattels mean that collecting antiques, rare books, paintings and similar items can be more tax-efficient than other investments and can make them particularly suitable as gifts. But bear in mind that the market for collectibles can be very fickle, making these high-risk investments, and the person you give them to is likely to incur costs storing and insuring these valuables.

- It has an expected life of more than 50 years, but the value of the item at the time you dispose of it is no more than £6,000.

If you give away or sell a decoration awarded (e.g. to you or a relative) for valour or gallantry, there is no CGT on any gain, unless you had originally bought the decoration or exchanged something of value for it.

Chattels worth more than £6,000

If a chattel's value is more than £6,000, any gain can be worked out in a special way, which may reduce the CGT bill (see Chapter 3). There are rules to prevent you reducing the CGT payable by splitting up a set – for example, a set of chairs – and then giving all the parts of the set to the same person.

19

Motor vehicles

There is no CGT on gains from selling or giving away a private car (including vintage or classic cars), a motorbike or other private motor vehicle. This exemption can also apply to a vehicle used for business provided it was 'commonly used as a private vehicle'. However, the exemption does not stretch to vehicles that are not commonly used as private vehicles and are unsuitable for use in that way – so watch out if you are tempted by surplus Ministry of Defence tanks or similar exotica!

A vehicle you sell or give away might have a personalised or cherished number plate. The right to use the combination of letters and numbers shown on the plate is an 'intangible' asset that is not covered by the CGT exemption for motor vehicles. If the value of the vehicle you sell or give away includes an amount in respect of the personalised plate, you need to apportion the proceeds between the value of the vehicle and the value of the right to use the registration shown on the plate, and there could be CGT to pay on the latter.

Your home

There is normally no CGT to pay when you dispose of part, or all, of your only, or main, home.

This exemption automatically includes your garden provided your whole plot (house plus garden) comes to no more than half a hectare (about 1.25 acres). It covers giving away part of the garden while you retain the house, but not if it has ceased to be garden. For example, if you built a house in the garden and gave the house to your children, the gift would not be covered by the exemption. But you could give the children part of the garden free of CGT and leave them to develop the plot.

If your plot is larger than half a hectare, there is no automatic exemption and the garden is exempt only if its size is warranted by the nature of the house and deemed necessary for the reasonable enjoyment of the home. This can be hard to prove if you are disposing of part of the garden while keeping the home, since the act of disposal suggests that for 'reasonable enjoyment' you don't really need such a large garden after all. However, HM Revenue & Customs might accept that a gift of part of the garden is tax-free if made to a relative whose presence would not detract from your enjoyment of the rest of the garden.

If you have more than one home, you should nominate one as your main home for CGT purposes. A husband and wife or civil partners who live together can have only one main home between them. This is so even if they each spend a lot of time in separate homes, for example, because they live apart during the week for work purposes. Couples who are not married and not in a registered civil partnership can each have a separate main home even if they live mainly together in just one home.

You may lose part of the exemption if part of your home was set aside exclusively for business. The same applies if you let out part or all of your home, though in that case you might qualify for

Planning point

If you have more than one home and want to nominate one as your main home, you must make your nomination in writing to your tax office within two years of acquiring a second or further home. Once made, you can change the nomination if you want to. If you fail to make a nomination within the two-year time limit, your main home is determined on the facts – for example, where your post is sent, where you are registered to vote, and so on.

other reductions in your CGT bill. There may also be a CGT bill when you dispose of your home, if you have lived away for long periods.

Some investments

Gains on some investments are completely free from CGT: for example, National Savings & Investments products (including premium bonds), gilts, most corporate bonds, and investments held through an individual savings account (ISA) or a personal equity plan (PEP). ISAs and PEPs can't themselves be

Jargon buster

Individual savings account (ISA) Scheme introduced by the government in 1999 with tax incentives to encourage people to save more. Each year, you have an ISA allowance of £7,000, which can be invested in stockmarket investments, like shares. If you choose, up to £3,000 of your allowance can be invested in cash (in other words, savings accounts offered by banks, building societies and National Savings & Investments)

Personal investment plan (PEP) An earlier scheme with tax incentives to encourage investment in stockmarket investments. It was replaced by ISAs from April 1999 onwards

Enterprise investment scheme (EIS) A scheme to encourage investment in new and growing trading companies. You get income tax relief on the amount you invest and any gains are tax-free provided you hold the shares for at least three years. This is a high-risk investment and losses could outweigh any tax advantage

Venture capital trust (VCT) A scheme to encourage investment in new and growing trading companies. It aims to be slightly lower risk than an EIS by spreading your investment across a range of different companies. You get income tax relief on the amount you invest provided you hold the shares for at least five years and any gains are tax-free

Case Study Frank and Janette

Frank and Janette have retired and plan to move permanently to their second home, which is in Devon and up to now they have just spent holidays and some weekends there. They want to give the family home in Kent to their only daughter, Marie.

The home is worth about £600,000 but there will be no CGT on the gift because the house has been Frank and Janette's main home throughout the whole time they have owned it. However, Frank and Janette will need to consider the IHT position of this gift (see Chapter 3).

21

transferred to someone else – you would need to sell the investments held within the ISA or PEP and give away the proceeds.

Provided certain conditions are met, gains on shares bought through an **Enterprise Investment Scheme** (EIS) or **Venture Capital Trust** (VCT) are also free of CGT.

Insurance policies

Payment from a life insurance policy, whether on maturity, early surrender or even through selling the policy to someone else, is usually exempt from CGT. The exemption does not apply, however, if you bought the policy from someone else, for example through an auction.

Your rights to certain payments

If you dispose of your right to receive an income under an annuity or a covenant, say, there is usually no CGT on any gain you make as a result. Similarly, if you give away your right to benefit under the terms of a trust or your right to repayment of money you have lent someone, there is usually no CGT – but there could be, if in the first place you had bought these rights.

❝ Gifts between a husband and wife or between civil partners are free of CGT provided the couple are living together. ❞

TAX-FREE TRANSACTIONS

Some types of transaction (regardless of the type of asset involved) are exempt from CGT or subject to other rules that mean there is no tax bill at the time of making a gift.

Gifts between husband and wife or between civil partners

Gifts between a husband and wife or between civil partners are free of CGT provided the couple are living together. The gift is not exempt but is treated as being made on a no-gain-no-loss basis – see Chapter 3 for an explanation of how this works.

Gifts to charities and certain other bodies

Donations and gifts to charity, and to various other institutions, including many

Case Study Rasheed

Rasheed wants to make a large donation to the local hospice which cared for his wife up to her death. He has some units in a unit trust on which he has made a substantial gain. If he sold the units and donated the proceeds to the charity, he would have to use part of the proceeds to pay CGT on the gain. But, if he transfers the units direct to the charity, this is a tax-free gift. There are also income tax advantages to making the donation in this way (see Chapter 6).

22

museums and art galleries, local authorities, government departments and universities, and, since 6 April 2002, community amateur sports clubs are CGT-free.

Gifts of national heritage property

The sale or gift of certain property, such as works of art, to a museum, art gallery, the National Trust or similar body, university, local authority or government department, may be exempt from CGT. So, too, is the acceptance by HMRC of such property in lieu of IHT (see page 26).

Eligible property can include pictures, prints, books, manuscripts, works of art and scientific objects, provided they are 'pre-eminent' for their national, scientific, historic or artistic interest. Buildings and land of outstanding scenic, historic or scientific interest and items associated with them are also eligible.

A gift of eligible property to anyone else can be free of CGT if it also qualifies as conditionally exempt from IHT (see page 26) or would do so if it did not count as a potentially exempt transfer (see Chapter 3).

To qualify, the person receiving the gift must agree certain conditions with HMRC including that the gifted property will stay in the UK, it will be properly maintained and preserved, and the public will have reasonable access to it. The exemption from CGT is lost if the property is subsequently sold, unless this is to a museum, art gallery, the National Trust or similar body, university,

local authority or government department.

If the gift is not exempt, you might instead be able to claim hold-over relief (see page 59).

Gifts if you move abroad

Since 17 March 1998, if you leave the UK to take up residence abroad, you can give away assets you acquired while still in the UK without paying any CGT, provided you count as a non-UK-**resident** and not **ordinarily resident** for at least five complete tax years. (But check

Jargon buster

Resident You will always count as resident in the UK if you spend 183 days or more of the tax year in the UK. You may still count as resident even if you spend fewer days here

Ordinarily resident This normally applies if you live in the UK year after year, even if you are away temporarily

Non-resident and not ordinarily resident This is likely to apply if you go to work full-time abroad and the following conditions are met: your absence from the UK and your contract of employment both last at least a whole tax year; your visits back to the UK add up to less than 183 days in any one tax year; and your visits back to the UK average 91 days per tax year or less. By concession, a husband, wife or civil partner accompanying their spouse to work abroad can also count as non-resident. If you go abroad for reasons other than work – say, you retire abroad – to count as non-resident, you will need to convince HM Revenue & Customs that you have severed your ties with the UK

23

whether you will be subject to any foreign tax in the new country where you become resident.) If your time abroad comes to less than five years, capital gains realised while you were away are subject to CGT in the tax year you return to the UK.

Gifts on death

When you die, you are deemed to make a gift of everything you own to your heirs but, whatever, and however much, you leave, it is always free of CGT. Your heirs are treated as acquiring the assets at their market value at the time of your death, so any previous capital gains that had built up while the assets were in your hands are wiped out.

❝ When you die, however much you leave, it is always free of CGT. Any previous gains that had built up while the assets were in your hands are wiped out. ❞

For more information about residency status, see HM Revenue & Customs booklet IR20 *Residents and non-residents* from tax offices or www.hmrc.gov.uk.

24

Inheritance tax

Most lifetime gifts you make are either free of inheritance tax (IHT) or count as potentially exempt transfers (PETs).

IHT is a tax on a 'transfer of value' from one person to another – in other words, a transaction that reduces the value of the estate of the person making the gift. In theory, IHT could apply to any gift but, as with CGT, there are exemptions. This means that on most lifetime gifts there is no IHT to pay, because:

- Various types of gift are always free of IHT.
- Some gifts, called 'potentially exempt transfers' (PETs), are free of tax, provided the giver lives on for seven years after making the gift (see Chapter 3).

❝ Most lifetime gifts you make are either free of IHT or count as potentially exempt transfers (PETs). ❞

Inheritance-tax-free gifts at a glance

The following gifts are tax-free. Conditions may apply and are explained in this chapter.

Tax-free in lifetime and on death
- Gifts between husband and wife or civil partners
- Gifts to charities and some similar bodies
- Gifts of national heritage property
- Gifts to political parties
- Gifts to housing associations

Tax-free lifetime gifts
- Normal expenditure out of income
- Gifts for the maintenance of your family
- Lottery syndicates and similar arrangements
- Yearly tax-free exemption
- Small gifts
- Wedding gifts
- Potentially exempt transfers if you survive seven years

 For information about which gifts count as PETs and how they are taxed, see page 57.

25

GIFTS THAT ARE ALWAYS FREE OF INHERITANCE TAX

The scope of IHT is, on the face of it, wider than that of CGT because IHT covers all assets – including money, as well as houses, land, pictures, furniture and investments. Gifts made in certain circumstances or between certain people or bodies are free of IHT. This applies to the following gifts, whether you make them during your lifetime or as bequests in your will (see Chapter 8).

Gifts between husband and wife or between civil partners

Gifts between husband and wife or between civil partners up to any amount are tax-free as long as the couple are not divorced (or the partnership hasn't been dissolved). Even a husband and wife or civil partners who are separated benefit from this exemption. If the husband, wife or civil partner receiving the gift is not 'domiciled' in the UK, the exemption is limited to a total of £55,000.

Jargon buster

Domicile Your place of domicile is broadly where you make your permanent home and intend to end your days. However, for the purposes of IHT, you are treated as still UK-domiciled during the first three years after you have acquired a domicile in another country, or if you have been a UK resident for 17 of the last 20 tax years

Gifts to charities and certain other bodies

This exemption from IHT is similar to the equivalent one for CGT (see page 22). It covers outright donations and gifts of any amount to UK charities, national museums and art galleries, universities, local authorities, government departments and a number of other bodies, including, since 6 April 2002, community amateur sports clubs.

Gifts of national heritage property

The gift of certain property, such as works of art, to a museum, art gallery, the National Trust or similar body, university, local authority or government department may be exempt from IHT. The transfer of such property to the HM Revenue & Customs in lieu of paying IHT (see page 176) is also exempt.

Eligible property can include pictures, prints, books, manuscripts, works of art and scientific objects, provided they are 'pre-eminent' for their national, scientific, historic or artistic interest. Buildings and land of outstanding scenic, historic or scientific interest and items associated with them are also eligible.

A gift of eligible property to anyone else can be conditionally exempt from IHT. To qualify, the person receiving the gift must agree certain conditions with HM Revenue & Customs, including that the gifted property will stay in the UK, it will be properly maintained and preserved, and the public will have reasonable access to it.

You can't claim conditional exemption for a gift that is a potentially exempt transfer (see page 57) but you can apply if the gift subsequently becomes chargeable because the giver died within seven years.

A claim for conditional exemption must be made within two years of the gift (or death in the case of a potentially exempt transfer). You (and/or your husband or wife) must have either owned the property for at least six years or inherited it on the death of the previous owner with a conditional exemption also applying to that transfer.

Gifts to political parties

A gift to a political party is exempt from IHT, provided the party has at least two MPs or polled at least 150,000 votes at the most recent general election.

Housing Associations

Gifts of land to a Registered Housing Association are exempt from IHT.

“If you can show the gift you are making is one of a regular pattern, the gift will be exempt from IHT. For example, you might pay a regular sum into a grandchild's child trust fund.”

LIFETIME GIFTS THAT ARE FREE OF INHERITANCE TAX

The following gifts are free of IHT only when they are made during your lifetime (so you can't get these exemptions for gifts you make through your will).

Normal expenditure out of income

If you can show that a gift you are making is one of a regular pattern of similar gifts and that you are making it out of your income (rather than from your savings or other capital), the gift will be exempt from IHT. For example, you might pay a regular sum each month into a grandchild's child trust fund.

Normally, gifts under this exemption are cash. If you make gifts that are not cash, you will have to be able to prove that the things you are giving were bought out of your current income.

Gifts made under a legally binding agreement, such as a deed of covenant, will usually be treated as regular gifts. So too will premiums you pay for an insurance policy or contributions to a pension scheme that is for the benefit of someone else: for example, a policy on your life, which would pay out to your children in the event of your death. If the gifts are not made under any formal agreement but you intend that they will be regular gifts, they can still qualify for the exemption.

The gifts do not necessarily have to be regular payments to one person. They could form a regular pattern of giving to different people – for example, gifts to each of your grandchildren on their

27

coming of age or large gifts to each of your children on their marriage (smaller gifts would be covered by the wedding exemption – see page 31).

HM Revenue & Customs decide each case on its merits. Usually it gets involved only after death when the personal representatives of someone who has died are claiming the exemption for gifts made within the seven years before death. But occasionally you might want to establish with HMRC during your lifetime that your gifts will form a regular pattern. If that is not clear at the time of the first few gifts, HM Revenue & Customs might agree provisionally to allow you the exemption, but they will review your case later on to see if you really have carried on making gifts as you intended.

The gifts must be made out of your current income and you must be able to show that you have enough income left to meet your day-to-day living expenses. The income can be from any source – a job, interest from investments, dividends from shares. However, for this purpose, not all receipts that you consider to be income are, in fact, income. For example, if you have bought a **purchased life annuity**, part of the 'income' you get counts as return of your capital so cannot be used to fund gifts under this IHT exemption. Similarly, some life insurance-based investments (such as with-profits

bonds and single premium bonds) let you withdraw each year up to 5 per cent of the amount you have invested as an 'income', but again this is not income for the purpose of this IHT exemption.

Case Study Bahiya

Bahiya shares her home with her son, Maalik. She realises that when she dies, there is likely to be an IHT bill on her estate and that Maalik might be forced to sell their home to pay it. To avoid this situation, Bahiya pays £100 a month for a whole life insurance policy that will pay out a lump sum direct to Maalik on her death. He will then be able to use the sum to pay the IHT due. Because the policy is for Maalik's benefit, the premiums count as gifts from Bahiya. They are exempt gifts for IHT because Bahiya pays them regularly as part of her normal spending out of her income.

For more information about how your regular gifts might be treated for inheritance tax, call HM Revenue & Custom's Inheritance Tax and Probate Helpline on 0845 302 0900.

28

Gifts for the maintenance of your family

Money or things that you give to provide housing, food, education, or some other form of maintenance, for your husband or wife, civil partner, ex-husband or ex-wife, ex-civil partner, children or a dependent relative are all outside the IHT net.

As far as husband and wife or civil partners are concerned, the normal exemption for gifts between married couples and civil partners (see page 26) would usually apply rather than this exemption. But if the recipient husband, wife or civil partner is domiciled (see page 26) abroad, this exemption could be useful. This exemption will usually cover maintenance agreements made as a result of a marriage breakdown or dissolution of a civil partnership.

The definition of children is very wide, covering stepchildren, illegitimate and adopted children, but it does not extend to grandchildren. Usually a child is considered to be adult when he or she reaches the age of 18 but, if he or she goes on to full-time education or training after that age, the IHT exemption carries on. This means, for example, that money you give a student son or daughter to support them while at university is exempt from IHT.

A 'dependent relative' can be any relative of you or your husband or wife who is unable to maintain him or herself because of old age or infirmity. It also includes your mother or mother-in-law, even if not elderly or infirm, if they are widowed, separated or divorced. As a concession, this exemption is also extended to gifts to your mother if she is unmarried, provided she is financially dependent on you.

❝ Money or things that you give to maintain your children are outside the IHT net. Likewise, money you give a student son or daughter to support him or her while at university is exempt from IHT. ❞

Lottery syndicates and similar arrangements

There is no IHT to pay on the transfer of winnings to members of a syndicate set up to share wins from schemes such as the National Lottery and football pools, provided the money is shared out according to an agreement that was drawn up in advance of the win. The agreement could be just oral but it is better to have a written agreement. So, if you and your family or friends often

HM Revenue & Customs have withdrawn all their information leaflets about inheritance tax. Instead, their guidance is published on the internet at www.hmrc.gov.uk/cto/customerguide/page1.htm.

29

Case Study Graham

Graham, 70, has played the National Lottery every week since it started. He often talked about how he would share a big win with his two children and his sister. Even so, he was stunned when he won over £500,000. He gave £100,000 each to his sister and children. This was in line with the plan he had discussed, but it would have been better if he had written it down. There will be no problem if he survives seven years after making the gifts, but, if he dies within that time, HM Revenue & Customs may query with his personal representatives whether the gifts really were exempt and argue instead that they should be treated as potentially exempt transfers (that become taxable gifts on death within seven years).

daydream about how you would give each other part of a really big win, it might be a good idea to draw up a formal arrangement now.

" Every tax year you can give away £3,000-worth of gifts. This exemption is in addition to the other exemptions. "

Yearly tax-free exemption

Every tax year, you can give away £3,000-worth of gifts without their counting in any way for IHT purposes. This exemption is in addition to the other exemptions, so a gift that qualifies for some other exemption does not count towards the £3,000 annual limit.

If you do not use up the full exemption one year, you can carry it forward to the next year – but not to any subsequent year. This means that, if you used none of last year's exemption, you could make up to £6,000-worth of gifts this year that qualify for the exemption. Gifts always use up the exemption for the tax year in which they are made first before using up any carried-forward exemption.

Small gifts

You can make as many gifts as you like totalling up to £250 to each person, and these will be exempt. You cannot combine the small gift exemption with another exemption to give more than £250 to one person but you can, say, give £3,000 to one recipient and gifts of £250 to any number of other people.

This exemption will generally cover birthday and Christmas presents, and any other small gifts you make during the year.

 For details of how potentially exempt transfers (PETs) are taxed, see page 57.

30

Wedding and civil partnership gifts

As a parent, you can give up to £5,000 to the happy couple free of IHT. A grandparent (or other ancestor) can give up to £2,500. Anyone else can give up to £1,000. The bride and groom or partners can give up to £2,500 to each other, but this limit will not be relevant if both are domiciled in the UK, since the exemption for married couples and civil partners will apply – gifts between spouses and civil partners are tax-free.

The exemptions apply to each giver: for example, assuming both sets of parents of the bride and groom or partners were still living, the couple could receive a maximum of £20,000 from their parents IHT-free.

Usually, gifts under this exemption will be outright gifts. But the exemption can also apply to gifts put into trust for the benefit of the bride, groom or civil partners, their children or the husbands or wives of their children.

POTENTIALLY EXEMPT TRANSFERS

A potentially exempt transfer (PET) is a gift from one person to another (or to a few types of trust – see Chapter 4) that is not covered by some other IHT exemption. As long as the person making the gift survives for seven years after the date of the gift, there is no IHT to pay. If the giver dies within seven years, there may be a tax bill. PETs are looked at in detail in Chapter 3.

❝ The couple could receive a maximum of £20,000 from their parents IHT-free. ❞

31

Combining the exemptions

Usually saving IHT means triggering a CGT bill or vice versa, but some gifts are free of both taxes.

Some types of gift are specifically exempt from both CGT and IHT: for example, gifts to charities and museums and gifts of national heritage property. Other gifts will be completely tax-free as long as they fall within an IHT exemption and they comprise cash or other assets that are not liable for CGT. Chapter 3 describes other situations in which either CGT or IHT may not be payable. You can sometimes combine the CGT and IHT exemptions in these situations to ensure that your gifts are free of both taxes.

❝ You can sometimes combine the CGT and IHT exemptions to ensure your gifts are free of both taxes. ❞

Case Study   Jeffrey

Jeffrey gives his son, Tom, £4,000 in cash as a wedding gift to help him and his new wife buy a home of their own. There is no CGT on a gift of cash and no IHT on a wedding gift of this size.

Jeffrey also wants to give his youngest daughter, Ruth, a gift of similar value. She decides she would like to have a watercolour – a family heirloom – which is valued at £4,500. This counts as a chattel (see page 19) and, since its value is within the £6,000 limit, there is no CGT liability. The gift is a PET under the IHT rules and so, since Jeffrey is expected to live a good many years longer, the gift is likely to be completely free of IHT.

All but the smallest charities need to be registered. To check whether an organisation is a registered charity, see www.charity-commission.gov.uk for England and Wales and www.oscr.org.uk for Scotland.

Taxable lifetime gifts

If you give away something not covered by any of the exemptions described in the previous chapter, there is a risk of tax on the gift. But, by timing your gifts to make best use of the various reliefs and allowances, you may be able to reduce the tax bill or eliminate it altogether. The two main taxes you need to worry about are capital gains tax and inheritance tax. They work in very different ways.

3

How capital gains tax works

Capital gains are the profits you make as a result of something increasing in value during the time you have owned it. You are taxed on these gains when you dispose of the asset, which includes giving it away.

Changes were made to the capital gains tax (CGT) system from 6 April 1998. If you dispose of something you first started to own on or after that date, you need only concern yourself with the post-1998 rules. But if you started to own the asset before then, you also need to get to grips with indexation allowance (see page 38).

NO TAX TO PAY?

Chapter 2 looked at gifts that are specifically exempt from CGT. But even if your gift is not exempt – for example, if you are giving away shares, a second home or a valuable heirloom – there could still be no tax to pay, because of:

- **Taper relief**. This reduces the amount on which you are taxed in line with the length of time you have owned the asset. Taper relief applies from 6 April 1998 onwards, with the greatest relief given to the assets you have held the longest. Taper relief is especially generous if you are disposing of a business asset, which includes some types of investment.
- **Indexation allowance**. Increases in the value of an asset in line with inflation up to April 1998 are not taxed.

- **Losses**. You reduce gains by deducting losses made on other assets.
- **Tax-free allowance**. Everyone can make several thousands of pounds of gains each year, which are automatically tax-free.

See the illustration opposite, which shows how the taxable gain on something you give away can be reduced.

Your first step in working out what tax might be due is to calculate the **basic gain** on the asset you are giving away – use the calculator on page 36. What happens next depends on when you first acquired the asset.

ASSETS ACQUIRED ON OR AFTER 1 APRIL 1998

The basic gain (amount D in the calculator overleaf) is your '**chargeable gain**' if the answer is greater than zero or your '**allowable loss**' if the answer is less than zero.

If you have made a chargeable gain, you must deduct any losses you have made during the same tax year in which the gift is made (see page 42 for more about losses). You also deduct any losses brought forward from earlier tax years but no more than are needed to

34

Capital gains tax: an overview

Use this illustration to see how the value on which CGT is levied can be reduced

The asset you give away | Value of the asset at the time you started to own it | Increase in value during the time you have owned the asset

There may be tax on this part | Increase in value during the time you have owned the asset

But you take away any part of the gain due just to inflation up to April 1998 | Indexation allowance

And you subtract any losses you've made on other assets in the same year | Losses

You also subtract any losses on other assets carried forward from earlier years | Losses

You take away taper relief (see page 37), which increases with the length of time you have owned the asset since April 1998 | Taper relief

Last, you subtract your yearly tax-free allowance | Tax-free allowance

Tax is due only on the bit of the gain that is left. If there is nothing left, there is no tax

35

Basic gain calculator

Final value of the gift (A)
This will usually be the price you would have received if you had sold the asset on the open market.

A £ _____

Initial value of the gift (B)
This is the price you originally paid for it or its market value at the time you first became the owner.

B £ _____

Allowable expenses (C)
These are costs you incurred in acquiring and disposing of the asset (for example, commission paid to a broker, the cost of an expert valuation or solicitor's fees, stamp duty paid on the purchase of a property or shares) and any expenses associated with enhancing the value of the asset (e.g. adding an extension to a property), but not spending on maintenance and repairs.

C £ _____

THE BASIC GAIN (D)
Work out A – B – C to find the basic gain.

D £ _____

reduce your gains to the amount of the tax-free allowance (again, see page 42). What's left is your 'net chargeable gain'.

You do not necessarily pay tax on the whole of your net chargeable gain, because you can deduct taper relief. In general, the longer you have held the asset, the more taper relief you get. For non-business assets – see the table, opposite – there is no reduction until you have held the asset for three years. The reduction then depends on the number of complete years since 6 April 1998 (inclusive) for which you have held the asset.

Taper relief is more generous if the asset you are giving away counts as a business asset (see page 62).

If you don't know the initial value of the item you are giving away, a professional valuer may be able to help, for example, a member of the National Association of Valuers and Auctioneers (see www.nava.org.uk). For quoted shares, use a historic share price service (for example, www.londonstockexchange.com). There is a charge for these services.

36

CGT taper relief for non-business assets

If you have held the asset for this many complete years after 5 April 1998:	Your net chargeable gain is reduced by this percentage:	Only this percentage of your gain counts as chargeable:	For example, a net chargeable gain of £1,000 is reduced to:
0	No reduction	100%	£1,000
1	No reduction	100%	£1,000
2	No reduction	100%	£1,000
3	5%	95%	£950
4	10%	90%	£900
5	15%	85%	£850
6	20%	80%	£800
7	25%	75%	£750
8	30%	70%	£700
9	35%	65%	£650
10 or more	40%	60%	£600

Case Study   Carole

Carole bought a holiday cottage in May 1998 for £65,000. The buying costs amounted to £1,200. In August 1998, she added a conservatory at a cost of £1,700. In June 2007, Carole gave the cottage to her niece. It was then valued at £125,000 and the costs incurred in making the transfer amounted to £1,500. Carole is deemed to have made a chargeable gain on the gift as follows:

Final value of the cottage	£125,000
less initial value	£65,000
less allowable expenses (£1,200 + £1,700 + £1,500)	£4,400
Chargeable gain	£55,600
less allowable losses	£0
Net chargeable gain before CGT taper relief	£55,600
Number of complete years for which cottage held (May 1998 to June 2007)	9 years
Percentage taper	65%
Net chargeable gain after taper relief (65% x £55,600)	£36,140

ASSETS ACQUIRED BEFORE 1 APRIL 1998 BUT AFTER 31 MARCH 1982

If you give away an asset that you started to own on or after 31 March 1982 but before 1 April 1998, work out the basic gain using the calculator on page 36. Next, divide your period of ownership into two:

- **Holding period 1:** From the date you started to own the asset up to April 1998.
- **Holding period 2:** From 6 April 1998 up to the date when you make the gift.

Holding period 1: indexation allowance

In respect of holding period 1 (date of acquisition up to April 1998), you can deduct indexation allowance (see page 41). Take the initial value of the asset and each allowable expense and multiply each of these values by the appropriate indexation factor (see the table on pages 202–3). Add the results together and the total is the indexation allowance.

Indexation allowance strips out any gains that are simply the result of inflation and do not represent any real increase in your wealth. However, the indexation allowance can at most wipe out the whole gain – it cannot be used to create or increase a loss for CGT purposes.

Deducting the indexation allowance from your basic gain gives you your **'indexed gain'**.

Holding period 2: taper relief

Having found your indexed gain, you next work out how much taper relief you qualify for in respect of holding period 2 (6 April 1998 to the date of gift) using the rules already described on pages 36–7, but with one exception: you are allowed to add one extra year to the holding period for any non-business asset that you already owned on 17 March 1998 (the Budget day on which taper relief was announced) (see case study, opposite).

> **❝Indexation allowance strips out any gains that are simply the result of inflation and do not represent any real increase in your wealth. ❞**

The tables you need to work out indexation allowance are on pages 202-3.

Case Study Frederick

Frederick gives a portfolio of unit trusts to his son on his 18th birthday on 1 September 2007. Frederick originally bought the units in July 1991 for £4,700. They are now worth £12,300, so there could be CGT on the gift. To work out whether he has made a chargeable gain, Frederick makes the following calculations:

Final value of units	£12,300
less initial value	£4,700
less fee paid for investment advice when the units were bought	£150
Basic gain	£7,450
Initial value and allowable expenses incurred at time of acquisition	£4,850
Indexation factor (see page 203)	0.215
Indexation allowance for period to April 1998 (0.215 x £4,850)	£1,043
Indexed gain (£7,450 – £1,043)	£6,407
less allowable losses	£0
Net chargeable gain before taper relief	£6,407
Taper relief	
Number of complete years from 6 April 1998 for which asset held	9
Plus one year because asset acquired before 17 March 1998	10
Percentage taper (see page 37)	60%
Net chargeable gain after taper relief (60% x £6,407)	£3,844

ASSETS ACQUIRED BEFORE 1 APRIL 1982

Gains due to inflation were not always tax-free. The legislation taking them out of the CGT net is effective only from the end of March 1982 onwards. For an asset that you started to own before 1 April 1982, the sums are slightly different from those outlined in the previous section. There are two methods of calculating your chargeable gain, as follows. The table below shows how to interpret the results:

- **Method 1**: The initial value is usually taken to be the value of the asset on 31 March 1982, and the indexation allowance for the initial cost is based on inflation since that date. Any allowable expenses incurred before 31 March 1982 are ignored; allowable expenses after that date are indexed in the normal way.
- **Method 2**: Work out the chargeable gain based on the whole period you

have owned the asset including the pre-March 1982 period. In this case, the initial value is the actual value at the time you first acquired the asset. The indexation allowance can be worked out based on either the initial value or the asset's value on 31 March 1982 but adjusting for inflation only since March 1982.

Planning point

For assets acquired before 1 April 1982, you can choose to use just Method 1. If you do, all these assets will be covered by the election. The effect is as if you had sold all your assets on 31 March 1982 and immediately re-bought them. It will usually be worth making this choice if the values of all or most of your assets were higher on 31 March 1982 than they were at the time you first acquired them.

The chargeable gain on pre-1 April 1982 assets

Use this table to ascertain which is the more favourable method for CGT purposes (see above) unless you have opted to use only Method 1 (see Planning point)

If Method 1 results in a:	And Method 2 results in a:	Your chargeable gain/allowable loss is:
Gain	Gain	The smaller of the two gains
Loss	Loss	The smaller of the two losses
Gain	Loss	Zero
Loss	Gain	Zero
Gain or Loss	Zero	Zero

40

WORKING OUT YOUR INDEXATION ALLOWANCE

Indexation allowance is the relevant initial value or allowable expense multiplied by the appropriate indexation factor.

The indexation factor depends on the month when you first acquired the asset or incurred the expense. Before April 1998, the factor also varied according to the month in which you disposed of the asset. But, since indexation allowance now runs only up to April 1998, there is just one set of indexation factors that applies to all disposals you make from 6 April 1998 onwards. These are shown in the table on pages 202–3. Look along the left-hand or right-hand side to find the year in which you acquired the asset or incurred the expense; run your eye across to the column for the relevant month. This is the indexation factor you should use.

Occasionally, you might need to work out the indexation factor for a period ending before April 1998. You can work it out by using the Retail Prices Index (RPI). This index is a commonly used measure of the level of prices in the UK and the relevant figures are given on pages 204–5. It lists the RPI from March 1982 up to April 1998. The latest RPI figure you will need for CGT calculations is that for April 1998.

To work out the appropriate indexation factor, take the RPI figure for the later month you are considering – call this RD. Then take the RPI figure for the earlier month you are looking at or for March 1982, whichever is appropriate, and call

Case Study Christina

In September 2007, Christina gave her daughter some jewellery that she had inherited from her own mother in February 1990 when it was valued at £8,000. Christina needs to work out what indexation allowance she can claim for the period February 1990 to 31 March 1998. Using the table of indexation factors on pages 202–3, she finds the year 1990 along the left-hand side and runs across to the column for February. The entry tells her that the indexation factor to use is 0.353. The indexation allowance she can claim is 0.353 x £8,000 = £2,824.

this RI. Now make the following calculation:

$$\text{Indexation factor} = \frac{RD - RI}{RI}$$

Indexation factors are rounded to the nearest third decimal place.

Case Study Gerald

Gerald had 1,000 shares in Megabucks plc which he had bought in June 1982. In March 1988, he bought a further 2,000 shares in the same company. The two purchases are pooled to form a 'section 104 holding' (see page 45). Before the new shares can be added to the pool, Gerald must work out the indexation allowance clocked up for the 1,000 shares he already held from June 1982 to March 1988. He needs to know what indexation factor to use. From the table on pages 202-3, he finds the RPI for June 1982 (81.85) and for March 1988 (104.1). The indexation factor is: (104.1 - 81.85) / 81.85 = 0.272.

41

HOW MUCH TAX?

There is just one more allowance to consider, then you can work out your final tax bill.

Yearly tax-free allowance

If you are deemed to have made a chargeable gain on an asset you gave away, there could be some tax to pay, but not necessarily. Everyone has a tax-free allowance. This means the first slice of chargeable gains that you make each year is tax-free. In 2007–8, you can have net chargeable gains of £9,200 before any CGT becomes payable. The tax-free allowance for earlier years is shown in the table, below.

Yearly CGT allowance

Tax year	Tax-free allowance
2002–3	£7,700
2003–4	£7,900
2004–5	£8,200
2005–6	£8,500
2006–7	£8,800
2007–8	£9,200

Claiming allowable losses

If you make a loss on something that you give away or otherwise dispose of, you must set the loss against gains that you have made on other assets in the same tax year.

If your losses come to more than your gains for the tax year, you carry forward the unrelieved losses to future years. (You can't carry them back to earlier years – although, when you die, your executors can.)

If your losses come to less than your gains for the tax year, you must next deduct any losses you have brought forward from earlier years, but only to the extent that your net chargeable gains are reduced to the amount of your tax-free allowance. Any losses not used up continue to be carried forward to be relieved in future years.

❝ In 2007–8, you can have net chargeable gains of £9,200 before any CGT becomes payable. ❞

You can also view CGT rates and allowances on the HMRC website at www.hmrc.gov.uk/rates/cgt.htm.

You deduct any losses you are claiming before applying the CGT taper. This means that losses, as well as gains, are reduced by the taper relief. But you set off the losses in the way which benefits you most. This means, where you have gains on several disposals in the same tax year, setting losses against the gain(s) that qualify for the lowest taper relief.

Planning point

The tax rules force you to set losses against your chargeable gains for the same year. This means that taper relief and your tax-free allowance could be wasted. If you are planning to give away something on which you have made a capital loss, choose the timing of your gift carefully to maximise the reliefs and allowances you can claim each tax year – see case study below.

Case Study Sally

So far, in 2007-8, Sally has made capital gains before taper relief of £9,500 on which she can claim 20 per cent taper relief. In March 2008, Sally is planning to give her nephew some shares on which she is showing a loss of £1,300. The tax rules will require Sally to deduct the loss from her gains, leaving her with net gains of £8,200 for the year. This is within her tax-free allowance of £9,200, so there is no CGT to pay, but Sally has wasted the taper relief and part of her allowance.

Instead, Sally could delay making the gift for a month so that it falls into the next tax year. Her gains in 2007-8 are reduced to £9,500 x 80% = £7,600 by the taper relief. This is well within her tax-free allowance so there is still no CGT to pay.

The gift in 2008-9 creates £1,300 of allowable losses which Sally can either use against gains she makes that year or, if she has none, can be carried forward to set against Sally's gains in future years.

If you don't know the initial value, or the value on 31 March 1982, of the item you are giving away, a professional valuer may be able to help, for example, a member of the National Association of Valuers and Auctioneers (see www.nava.org.uk). For quoted shares, use a historic share price service, such as www.londonstockexchange.com.

Working out the tax bill

If, after deducting all your reliefs and allowances, you are left with a taxable gain, there will be CGT to pay. CGT is charged at three rates in 2007–8: 10 per cent, 20 per cent and 40 per cent. Add your taxable gains to your taxable income for the year and use the table below to see which tax rate(s) apply to your gain.

If your taxable income is below a threshold shown in the table and adding the gain to the income takes the total above the threshold, you will pay the lesser tax rate on part of your gain and the greater rate on the rest.

For example, if you have taxable income of £33,600 in the 2007–8 tax year and taxable gains of £2,500 (a total of £36,000), you would pay 20 per cent CGT on £1,000 of the gain and 40 per cent CGT on the £1,500 of gain above the higher-rate threshold.

Tax rate on chargeable gains 2007-8

If your gains plus taxable income equal:	This tax rate applies
Up to £2,230	10%
From £2,231 to £34,600	20%
More than £34,600	40%

Case Study Emily

In the 2007-8 tax year, Emily has net chargeable gains of £9,929. She deducts the tax-free slice of £9,200, leaving taxable gains of £829. Emily's taxable income for the year is £34,000. The tax on her gains is worked out as follows:

Part of gains in excess of £34,600 threshold	£229
Part of gains within basic-rate band	£600
CGT at 40% on £229	£ 91.60
CGT at 20% on £600	£120.00
Total CGT bill	£211.60

SPECIAL RULES FOR SOME TYPES OF ASSETS OR GIFTS

There are some additional rules to take into account if you are giving away shares, unit trusts or chattels, or you are making a gift to your husband, wife or civil partner.

❝You own shares in one company, all of the same type but bought at different times. Special rules are needed to identify which shares you are disposing of.❞

Shares and unit trusts

If you give away identical shares, unit trusts or other securities that you acquired all at the same time, the CGT rules apply in the same way as for any other asset. But suppose you own shares in one company, all of the same type but bought at different times. Special rules are needed to identify which shares you are disposing of, so that you can use the correct initial value, indexation allowance and taper relief.

For gifts and other disposals made on or after 6 April 1998, the shares you give away are matched to the ones you own in the following order:

- Shares you bought on the same day.
- Shares purchased within the following **30 days**. This rule was introduced to curb a practice called 'bed-and-breakfasting'. You used to be able to realise a capital gain or loss by selling shares one day and buying them back the next. Such a move could be very tax-efficient – for example, crystallising enough gain each year to use up your tax-free allowance. Now, you need to leave at least 30 days between selling the shares and buying them back.
- **Shares bought on or after 6 April 1998**, identifying with the most recent acquisitions first – this is called a last-in-first-out (LIFO) basis.
- **Shares in your 'section 104 holding'.** These are shares you acquired between 6 April 1982 and 5 April 1998 inclusive. These shares are pooled together. Your initial value and indexation allowance are worked out as a proportion of the values for all the shares in the pool. The calculation has to be reworked every time there is a change to the contents of the pool. ('Section 104' refers to the part of the tax legislation that sets out these rules.)
- **Shares in your '1982 holding'.** These are shares you acquired between 6 April 1965 and 5 April 1982 inclusive. Again, they form a pool and to value the shares you take a proportion of the value for the pool as a whole, which has to be recalculated every time the contents

45

of the pool change. The indexation allowance is calculated only from 31 March 1982.

- **Shares you acquired before 6 April 1965**, starting with the shares you bought most recently (LIFO basis). You can opt to have quoted shares treated as part of your 1982 holding.

66 The 30-day rule does not apply in the following circumstances: you sell shares you own direct and buy them back within an individual savings account ('bed-and-ISA'). 99

Planning point

The 30-day share-matching rule means you can no longer crystallise a capital gain or loss by selling shares one day and buying them back the next. But the 30-day rule does not apply in the following circumstances: you sell shares you own direct and buy them back within an individual savings account ('bed-and-ISA'); you sell shares you own and your spouse or civil partner buys the same shares; you sell shares in one company and buy shares in a different but very similar company. Using these techniques could help you wipe out some or all of a taxable gain before making a gift of the assets.

Case Study Connie

Connie received 300 Alliance & Leicester shares when the building society was demutualised in April 1997 and she bought further shares in the company as follows:

9 April 1998	1,700 shares
2 November 1999	500 shares
16 July 2000	700 shares

In October 2007, she decides to give half her Alliance & Leicester shares to her niece, Harriet. The 1,600 shares she gives away are matched in the following order:

16 July 2000	700 shares
2 November 1999	500 shares
9 April 1998	400 shares

Any subsequent gifts or other disposals would be matched against the remaining 1,300 shares bought on 9 April 1998 and then her original 300 shares.

Chattels

'Chattels' means personal possessions, such as pictures, furniture, antiques, jewellery and other collectibles.

There is no CGT on gifts of chattels with a predictable life of 50 years or less or on more durable chattels where they are valued at £6,000 or less (see Chapter 2). For chattels worth more than £6,000, special rules apply that can reduce the tax you pay. The chargeable gain is the lower of either five-thirds of the excess of the disposal value over £6,000 or the gain (before deducting any losses or taper relief but after deducting any indexation allowance) worked out in the normal way. Once the chargeable gain has been determined, any losses and taper relief are deducted in the usual way.

Gifts between husband and wife or between civil partners

There is no CGT on a gift between a husband and wife or between civil partners (see Chapter 2) and the transfer is said to be made on a no-gain-no-loss basis. What this means becomes important if the recipient subsequently sells or gives away the asset, because in order to work out any CGT bill, you need to know about the following:

- **Date of acquisition**. For CGT, the spouse or civil partner receiving the gift started to own the asset from the date of the gift.
- **Initial value**. The recipient is treated as if the value on that date is the initial

value which applied to the spouse or civil partner making the gift plus any allowable expenses and/or indexation allowance the giver qualified for. In effect, the recipient has taken over the giver's allowable expenses and indexation allowance.

- **Taper relief**. The period of ownership of the spouse or civil partner making the gift is added to the recipient's period of ownership for the purpose of calculating taper relief.

Case Study Samir

Samir bought a paddock for £5,000 in May 1996. His indexation allowance for the period May 1996 to April 1998 is 0.063 x £5,000 = £315. In October 2007, he gives the paddock to his wife, Mel. In January 2008, Mel sells the paddock for £12,000. To work out whether CGT is due, Mel needs to do the following calculations:

- Final value: £12,000.
- Deduct initial value: £5,315 (Samir's initial value plus Samir's indexation allowance and any allowable expenses).
- Deduct Mel's allowable expenses: £300 in solicitor's fees.
- This gives an indexed gain of: £12,000 - £5,315 - £300 = £6,385.
- Taper relief is based on Samir's and Mel's combined period of ownership since April 1998, in other words, nine complete years plus a bonus year because Samir already held the paddock on 17 March 1998 - see page 38 - making 10 years' taper relief in total, giving a tapered gain of 60% x £6,385 = £3,831.

47

TELLING THE TAXMAN

If you have taxable gains and you receive a full-length tax return, you need to complete the capital gains supplement. If your tax affairs are fairly straightforward, you may instead be sent a short four-page tax return. There is no place on the short return to report capital gains. You need either form R40(CG) or the full return instead.

To avoid penalties, file your 2007 tax return no later than 31 January 2008. This is also the deadline for paying any CGT. Your tax office will work out your tax bill for you, provided you get your return back by 30 September 2007. Alternatively, you can file your return online, in which case, the software should tell you how much tax you owe. The free HM Revenue & Customs software does not cover the CGT supplement, so you'll need to buy a commercial package (see below).

If you don't get a tax return, you must tell your tax office about any taxable capital gains by 5 October following the end of the tax year in which you made the gains. There is no need to report disposals if you have no tax to pay.

You must keep records of the information that backs up your return for one year following the date on which you filed the return (longer if you are in business). Your tax office can ask to see these records and fine you if you can't produce them.

From the 2008 tax return onwards, the tax deadlines are changing. The deadline for getting in your tax return online remains at 31 January (in other words, 31 January 2009 for the tax return covering the tax year 2007–8). But, if you are sending in a paper return, from the 2008 tax return onwards, the deadline is brought forward to 31 October - that is, 31 October 2008 for the 2007–8 tax return. The deadline for paying any tax due remains 31 January.

❝If you are sending in a paper return, from the 2008 tax return onwards, the deadline is brought forward to 31 October from 31 January.❞

Typically a commercial tax return package costs from, say, £12.50 up to £25. You can find a list of suitable software on the HM Revenue & Customs website at www.hmrc.gov.uk/efiling/sa_efiling/soft_dev.htm.

48

How inheritance tax works

Most lifetime gifts escape IHT. But some are taxable when
they are made and many become taxable if the giver dies.

Chapter 1 listed lifetime gifts that are
always free of IHT. Other gifts you make
will be either:

- **Taxable gifts** (more formally called
'chargeable transfers'). Following
changes in the 2006 Finance Act, this
now includes gifts to most types of
trust. This chapter explains how taxable
gifts are treated for IHT. See Chapter 4
for information about using trusts, or
- **Potentially exempt transfers (PETs),**
which mainly covers outright gifts to
people (but also gifts into trust for a
disabled person – see Chapter 4).

The value of a gift for IHT is the loss to
the giver (which may differ from the
value of the gift to the recipient).

TAXABLE GIFTS
The main lifetime gifts that are taxable
are most gifts to trusts. When you make
a taxable gift there may be a tax bill at
the time you make the gift. If you die
within the following seven years, the
recipient could also be charged extra tax.

How taxable gifts are taxed
IHT does not apply to each gift you
make in isolation. It is based on all the
taxable gifts you have made over the
last seven years. Adding all these gifts
together gives you a 'cumulative total'
– called your '**running total**' in this
book. The first slice of the running
total – up to £300,000 for the
2007–8 tax year – is tax-free. You pay
tax only on a gift (or part of it) that
spills over the tax-free limit – see the
illustration overleaf.

The tax-free limit is normally increased
each tax year broadly in line with price
inflation but the changes have sometimes
been more erratic. Exceptionally, the
government has announced in advance
the tax-free limits for the next few years
(though they could be revised) – see the
table on page 52.

The IHT rate on lifetime gifts is set at
half the rate of tax that may apply to
your estate when you die. The death rate
for the 2007–8 tax year is 40 per cent;
so the lifetime rate is 20 per cent.

HM Revenue & Customs have withdrawn all their information leaflets about
inheritance tax. Instead, their guidance is published on the internet at
www.hmrc.gov.uk/cto/customerguide/page1.htm.

49

Inheritance tax: an overview

The asset you give away

This may be a lifetime gift or your estate at death
(On death, what you leave is treated as your final gift)

If your current gift is taxable, it is added to any other taxable gifts you have made during the seven years up to the time of this gift

7 years

6 years

GIFT A

5 years

4 years

GIFT B

3 years

2 years

1 year

CURRENT GIFT

"IHT is based on all the taxable gifts you have made over the last seven years."

> **"The first slice of the running total is tax-free. You pay tax only on a gift (or part of it) that spills over the tax-free limit."**

You have a tax-free limit

← Tax-free limit (the nil-rate band) →

Taxable gifts over the last seven years use up the limit in the order the gifts were made

GIFT A | GIFT B | CURRENT GIFT

← Tax-free limit (the nil-rate band) →

If the current gift falls within the limit, no tax is due

GIFT A | GIFT B | CURRENT GIFT

← Tax-free limit (the nil-rate band) →

If part or all of the current gift falls above the limit, tax is due

GIFT A | GIFT B | CURRENT GIFT

← Tax-free limit (the nil-rate band) →

Taxable part of gift

51

Rates of inheritance tax

The tax-free limit is normally increased each year in line with inflation but increases for 2007-8 to 2009-10 have been set in advance and may turn out to be higher or lower than inflation. Since March 1988, the rates of tax for IHT have been unchanged.

IHT due on a lifetime gift at the time the gift is made can be paid either by the person or trust making the gift or by the person or trust receiving the gift. If the giver pays, the tax itself counts as part of the gift, increasing the value of the transfer to be taxed.

A gift where the giver pays the tax is called a '**net gift**'; if the recipient pays the tax, it is called a '**gross gift**'. You can work out how much tax is due on a net or gross gift using the calculators overleaf.

Jargon buster

Gross gift A gift where the person receiving the gift pays any tax due
Net gift A gift where the person making the gift pays any tax due
Nil-rate band Another name for the IHT-free limit

Death within seven years

Tax on a lifetime gift that is a chargeable transfer is usually charged at a rate of 20 per cent (in 2007-8). But, if the person making the gift dies within seven years, the gift is reassessed and tax is recalculated using the tax-free limit and death rate current at the time of death (£300,000 and 40 per cent for 2007-8). If the giver dies more than

Rates of inheritance tax

Tax year	Tax-free limit	Rate of tax on running total in excess of the tax-free limit	
		Death rate	Lifetime rate
2001-2	£242,000	40%	20%
2002-3	£250,000	40%	20%
2003-4	£255,000	40%	20%
2004-5	£263,000	40%	20%
2005-6	£275,000	40%	20%
2006-7	£285,000	40%	20%
2007-8	£300,000	40%	20%
2008-9	£312,000	Not yet announced	Not yet announced
2009-10	£325,000	Not yet announced	Not yet announced

Inheritance tax taper relief

Years between gift and death	% of full death rate which applies (at 2007-8 rates)	% rate of tax on the gift
Up to 3	100	40
More than 3 and up to 4	80	32
More than 4 and up to 5	60	24
More than 5 and up to 6	40	16
More than 6 and up to 7	20	8
More than 7	0	no extra tax

three years but less than seven years after making the gift, the full death rate is reduced by IHT taper relief – see above.

Various factors influence whether any extra tax might be due:

- Tax on the reassessed gift is worked out using the tax-free limit and death rate at the time of death. The tax-free limit will normally be higher than the limit that applied at the time of the gift. The death tax rate will normally be higher than the lifetime rate but this will not necessarily be so if the government has since changed the rates.

- PETs made within seven years of death are reclassified as taxable gifts (see page 57). If they were made before the taxable gift being reassessed, the PETs will now use up part of the tax-free limit that had previously been available for the taxable gift.

Any extra tax due will be charged to the person who received the gift but, if they cannot or will not pay, the giver's estate must pay. There is no refund if the reassessed tax bill is lower than the original amount of tax paid.

As well as extra tax on the gift, death within seven years may increase tax on your estate. See page 160 for an example of how lifetime gifts can affect tax on your estate at death.

Inheritance tax calculator for a net gift (2007-8)

A net gift is when the giver pays the tax.

Running total before your latest gift (A)
Add up all the taxable gifts you have made during the last seven years. If you paid the IHT on any of those gifts, include the tax you paid.

A £ _____

Tax on your running total (B)
If amount A is £300,000 or less, tax is £0. If amount A is greater than £300,000, tax is 20% of the excess, in other words, 20% x (A - £300,000).

B £ _____

Your net running total (C)
Work out A - B.

C £ _____

Your current gift (D)
Enter the value of the gift you are now making. Use the amount that the recipient will receive.

D £ _____

Your new running total (E)
Work out C + D.

E £ _____

Tax on your new running total (F)
If amount E is £300,000 or less, tax is £0. If amount E is greater than £300,000, tax is 25% [1] of the excess, in other words, 20% x (E - £300,000).

F £ _____

TAX ON THE CURRENT GIFT (G)

Work out F - B to find the amount of tax to be paid by the giver on the current gift.

G £ _____

[1] This percentage is derived as follows. The gross value of the gift is found by dividing the net gift by (1 - 20%): a process called grossing up. To find the tax due on the gift, the grossed-up value is multiplied by the lifetime IHT rate of 20%. But 20%/(1 - 20%) = 20%/80% = 25%, so we can simply multiply the net gift by 25%.

54

Inheritance tax calculator for a gross gift (2007-8)

A gross gift is when the recipient pays the tax.

Running total before your latest gift (A)
Add up all the taxable gifts you have made during the last seven years. If you paid the IHT on any of those gifts, include the tax you paid.

A £ _____

Tax on your running total (B)
If amount A is £300,000 or less, tax is £0. If amount A is greater than £300,000, tax is 20% of the excess, in other words, 20% x (A - £300,000).

B £ _____

Your current gift (C)
Enter the value of the gift you are now making. Use the amount that you are giving.

C £ _____

Your new running total (D)
Work out A + C.

D £ _____

Tax on your new running total (E)
If amount D is £300,000 or less, tax is £0. If amount D is greater than £300,000, tax is 20% of the excess, in other words, 20% x (E - £300,000).

E £ _____

TAX ON THE CURRENT GIFT (F)
Work out E - B to find the amount of tax to be paid by the recipient on the current gift.

F £ _____

55

Case Study | Frederick 1

Frederick wants to set up a discretionary trust to make sure that his two grown-up children and any future grandchildren will have a 'last resort' emergency fund to help them out if the need arises. (For more about discretionary trusts, see Chapter 4.)

Frederick sets up the trust on 1 October 2007 with a gift of £70,000. He will pay any tax due on this, so it is a net gift. As Frederick has not used any of his annual exemption of £3,000 for 2007–8 (see page 30), only £67,000 is taxable. Over the seven years from 2 October 2000 to 1 October 2007, he has made other taxable gifts of £250,000. He uses the calculator for net gifts on page 54 to work out his IHT position as follows:

- **Amount A:** Frederick's running total before making the gift is £250,000
- **Amount B:** The running total is less than £300,000 so the tax on it is £0
- **Amount C:** The net running total is £250,000
- **Amount D:** He enters the value of gift, using the amount the trust will receive: £67,000
- **Amount E:** Adding C and D gives a new net running total of £317,000
- **Amount F:** Tax on the new running total is 25% x (£317,000 – £300,000) = £4,250
- **Amount G:** Subtracting B from F comes to £4,250 – £0 = £4,250. This is the amount of tax to be paid by Frederick on the gift to the trust.

Frederick's gift to the trust is made up of the £70,000 plus the £4,250 he pays in tax, making £74,250 in total.

Case Study | Frederick 2

Suppose, in the previous case study, Frederick decided to give £70,000 to the trust, but leave the trust to pay any tax. The taxable gift of £67,000 would be a gross gift. Using the calculator on page 55 for gross gifts, the IHT position would be:

- **Amount A:** Frederick's running total before making the gift is £250,000
- **Amount B:** The running total is less than £300,000 so the tax on it is £0
- **Amount C:** He enters the value of gift, using the amount he is giving: £67,000
- **Amount D:** Adding A and C gives a new net running total of £317,000
- **Amount E:** Tax on his new running total is 20% x (£317,000 – £300,000) = £3,400
- **Amount F:** Subtracting B from E comes to £3,400 – £0 = £3,400. This is the amount of tax to be paid by the trust

The trust would receive £70,000 but £3,400 would have to be used to pay the IHT bill due on the transfer, leaving £66,600 in the trust fund.

56

POTENTIALLY EXEMPT TRANSFERS (PETS)

Gifts that are neither exempt (see Chapter 2) nor taxable are potentially exempt transfers (PETs). They are initially treated as exempt but, if you die within seven years, the clock is turned back and the PET reassessed as a taxable gift. This can have several effects:

- **The gift**. There may be a tax bill on the PET itself.
- **Other gifts**. The PET may become part of the running total of other PETs and taxable gifts made in the seven years before death, so extra tax might become due on them (see page 53).
- **The estate**. The PET becomes part of the running total of gifts made in the seven years before death, so may cause extra tax on the estate (see Chapter 7).

How the PET is taxed

If the giver dies within seven years, the PET is treated as if it had originally been a taxable gift. This does not necessarily mean tax becomes due, because of:

- **The yearly tax-free exemption**. If the exemption (see page 30) has not already been used, up to £3,000 (or £6,000 if the previous year's exemption is also unused) of the reclassified PET is tax-free.
- **The tax-free limit**. Only if the running total of gifts in the seven years up to the PET exceeds the relevant tax-free limit will any tax become due. In the case of a reassessed PET, the relevant tax-free limit is the amount in force at the time of death (not at the time the gift was made). The limit is £300,000 if the giver died in the 2007–8 tax year.

If the running total up to the making of the reassessed PET does come to more than the tax-free limit, IHT is due at the rate current at the time of death (40 per cent in 2007–8). However, if the giver died more than three years after making the gift, tax is reduced by IHT taper relief – see the table, below.

Any tax that becomes due on a reassessed PET is first charged to the person who received the gift. If they

How IHT taper relief reduces tax on a reassessed PET

Years between making the PET and death	% of full death rate which applies (at 2007-8 rates)	% rate of tax on the gift
Up to 3	100	40
More than 3 and up to 4	80	32
More than 4 and up to 5	60	24
More than 5 and up to 6	40	16
More than 6 and up to 7	20	8
More than 7	0	no extra tax

> **!** Taper relief only reduces any tax on the reassessed PET. If there is no tax on the PET (for example, because the running total including the PET, is less than the tax-free limit), then taper relief has no relevance. Taper relief cannot be used to reduce tax on the estate of the deceased giver.

don't pay, the late giver's estate must pay the bill.

Note that PETs in the *seven years before death* are reassessed. Taxable gifts in the *seven years up to the making of the PET* are looked at in deciding whether tax is due. This means that gifts made during the 14 years before death could be relevant.

Case Study Godfrey

Godfrey dies on 1 January 2008. He made the following gifts during his lifetime (assume the annual tax-free exemption has already been used each year):

1 January 1998	Taxable gift	£100,000 to a discretionary trust
1 January 2000	Taxable gift	£70,000 to a discretionary trust
1 February 2001	Taxable gift	£68,000 to a discretionary trust
1 June 2003	PET	£80,000 to his nephew, John

On his death, taxable gifts and PETs made within the last seven years (2 January 2001 to 1 January 2008) are reassessed as follows:

- **Taxable gift on 1 February 2001.** Tax was originally paid in 2000-1 on a running total of £100,000 + £70,000 + £68,000 = £238,000. The tax-free limit then was £234,000 and the trust paid tax at 20 per cent on the £4,000 of the gift that exceeded the limit: 20% x £4,000 = £800. When the gift is reassessed on Godfrey's death, there is no extra tax due because the running total of £238,000 is less than the tax-free limit of £300,000 in force at the time of death.

- **PET on 1 June 2003.** No tax was charged on the PET at the time it was made. When it is reassessed on Godfrey's death, the PET becomes the top slice of £80,000 on a running total of £100,000 + £70,000 + £68,000 + £80,000 = £318,000. As the tax-free limit is £300,000, this leaves £18,000 of the PET to be taxed at the death rate of 40 per cent. So tax is initially calculated as 40% x £18,000 = £7,200. However, taper relief applies because the PET was more than three years before Godfrey's death. Only 60 per cent of the tax is payable - i.e. 60% x £7,200 = £4,320.

 Either the giver or the recipient of a PET can take out insurance to cover a tax bill expected to arise if the giver dies within seven years - see Chapter 7.

FALL IN VALUE OF A TAXABLE GIFT OR A PET

There is some tax relief if the value of a reassessed PET or taxable gift has fallen since the time it was first made. (This applies regardless of the type of gift – for example, land, chattels, shares, and so on.) Whoever is paying the tax is allowed to deduct the fall in value from the original value of the gift. Bear in mind that the original value of a gift was the loss to the giver not the value to the recipient, so even a large percentage fall in the value of the item in the recipient's hands might have only a small impact on the value of the item for IHT purposes.

HOLD-OVER RELIEF

With some gifts, you could face bills for both CGT and IHT at the time you make them. Hold-over relief lets you avoid a double tax bill, by, in effect, giving away your CGT too. Gifts that qualify include:

- Gifts that count as taxable gifts for IHT.
- Gifts that would count as taxable if they were not covered by the yearly tax-free exemption (see page 30) or the tax-free limit (see page 52).
- PETs if they become chargeable because the giver dies within seven years.

" Hold-over relief lets you avoid a double tax bill, by, in effect, giving away your CGT too. "

Case Study **Dorothy**

In September 2005, Dorothy gave her niece, Charlotte, one of a pair of antique vases. As a pair, they had a market price of £110,000 but individually were each worth only £40,000. Therefore the value of the gift was £110,000 – £40,000 = £70,000. The gift counted as a PET.

In February 2008, Dorothy dies and Charlotte receives a demand for tax on the gift. She has the vase valued and it is now worth £35,000. Charlotte agrees to the reduced value of the gift which is £70,000 – £5,000 = £65,000.

Dorothy's running total of gifts up to September 2005 was £240,000. Adding the value of the vase brings the total to £240,000 + £65,000 = £305,000. This is £5,000 more than the 2007-8 tax-free limit of £300,000, so Charlotte must pay tax of 40% x £5,000 = £2,000. As fewer than three years have passed since the gift, taper relief does not apply.

To claim the fall-in-value relief, contact HMRC Inheritance Tax – see page 210 for contact details. For more information about hold-over relief, see HM Revenue & Customs Helpsheet IR295, available from 0845 9000 404 or www.hmrc.gov.uk/sa, which includes a claim form.

59

The chargeable gain you have made on the gifted asset is deducted from your total chargeable gains for the year, so you pay no CGT on the gift. The chargeable gain is also deducted from the recipient's initial value, which increases the likelihood of a chargeable gain when the recipient comes to dispose of the gift. The recipient's taper relief is calculated from the date they became the new owner of the asset.

You can't claim hold-over relief if you are making the gift to a trust in which you have an interest (called a 'settlor-interested trust' – see Chapter 4).

" You do not have to tell the authority about lifetime gifts you make that count as PETs, but you should keep a record of them. "

TELLING THE TAXMAN

You do not have to tell the tax authorities about lifetime gifts you make that count as PETs, but you should keep a record of them. Put the record where it would be found by whoever would handle your estate if you were to die, since they will be required to check what gifts you have made in the seven years prior to death and to report them for tax purposes.

If you make taxable gifts you don't need to tell the Revenue if:

- Your total taxable gifts for the year come to no more than £10,000 and
- your running total of gifts over the last ten (not seven) years comes to no more than £40,000.

If you do need to report a taxable gift, use form IHT100 (see below). Normally you must send in the form within 12 months of the end of the month in which you made the gift but any tax due must usually be paid before this. With a lifetime taxable gift, tax is normally due within six months of the end of the month the gift was made. But if the gift was made in the period 6 April to 30 September, tax is due by 30 April of the following year.

If tax is due on a PET or taxable gift following the death of the giver within seven years, the tax is due within six months of the end of the month in which death occurred.

 Form IHT100 is available from HMRC Inheritance Tax (see page 210) or downloadable from the website www.hmrc.gov.uk/cto.

Giving away business assets

Some investments count as business assets for CGT and IHT and so benefit from favourable tax treatment.

Advice on giving away your business, farm or woodland is outside this book's scope. You should seek professional advice from a solicitor or accountant. But some fairly ordinary investments count as business assets and this section outlines how they are taxed when you give them away.

CAPITAL GAINS TAX AND BUSINESS ASSETS

A gift of business assets may qualify for extra reliefs from CGT.

Hold-over relief

Gifts of business assets qualify for hold-over relief. This applies even if there is no immediate IHT bill on the gift (see page 59), for example, where you are giving the business asset to an individual. How hold-over relief works is described opposite. The effect is that you give away your CGT liability with the gift.

The definition of business assets includes shares in unlisted trading companies. Importantly for investors, a company counts as unlisted even if it is quoted on the Alternative Investment Market (AIM). 'Trading company' is a company carrying

on one or more trades, professions or vocations in order to make a profit. It excludes simply holding investments (except where they do not make up a substantial extent of the company's activities). 'Trading company' specifically includes letting out furnished holiday accommodation on a commercial basis, which could be useful if you want to give away a holiday home to your children, say.

For more information about hold-over relief, see HM Revenue & Customs Helpsheet IR295, available from 0845 9000 404 or www.hmrc.gov.uk/sa, which includes a claim form.

61

Taper relief

Page 36 looks at the way taper relief can reduce the amount of CGT you may have to pay on a gift. If you give away business assets (and don't want to claim hold-over relief), a higher than normal rate of taper relief applies in respect of periods since April 1998 during which you owned the asset. Taper relief for business assets was made more generous for disposals from 6 April 2000 and again from 6 April 2002 – the table below shows the rates that apply from 6 April 2002 onwards.

The definition of business assets applicable for taper relief includes furnished holiday lettings and shares in a qualifying company. The definition of 'qualifying company' changed from April 2000 (see the box, below) and now

CGT taper relief for business assets

If you have held the asset for this many complete years after 5 April 1998:	Your net chargeable gain is reduced by this percentage:	Only this percentage of your gain counts as chargeable:	For example, a net chargeable gain of £1,000 is reduced to:
0	No reduction	100%	£1,000
1	50%	50%	£500
2 or more	75%	25%	£250

What is meant by 'qualifying company'?

These definitions relate to some instances where the higher taper relief for business assets may apply.

For periods before 6 April 2000 it meant:
- A trading company where you controlled at least 25 per cent of the voting rights, or
- Provided you were a full-time officer or employee of the company, a trading company where you controlled at least 5 per cent of the voting rights.

From 6 April 2000 onwards it means:
- Any unlisted trading company (including trading companies quoted on AIM)
- A quoted trading company where you control at least 5 per cent of the voting rights, or
- Provided you are an officer or an employee (full- or part-time), any quoted company whether a trading or non-trading company. If non-trading, you must not control more than 10 per cent of the voting rights, income or assets.

62

includes AIM-quoted trading companies and most shares you acquire through an employee share scheme at work. So, if you have these types of investment, they could make particularly tax-efficient gifts.

If you give away an asset that counted as a non-business asset for part of the time you owned it, but a business asset for the rest of the time, you have to apportion any capital gain between the two periods and claim the relevant taper relief for each part. Perversely, this can mean a higher tax bill than on an asset that you have held for longer but which counted as a business asset for the whole period (see the case study below).

Case Study Bella and Richard

Since 6 April 1998, Bella has held 3 per cent of the ordinary shares of Hammerson Ltd, an unquoted electronics company. Until 6 April 2000, this holding did not count as a business asset but from that date it does.

On 10 May 2007, Bella decides to give the shares to her granddaughter, Phoebe. She realises a taxable profit of £12,000. For taper relief purposes, she has held the shares for nine complete years. This entitles her to 35 per cent taper relief at the non-business rate (see page 37) and 75 per cent at the business taper rate.

During seven of these nine years (6 April 2000 to 5 April 2007), the shares counted as a business asset. Therefore, business taper relief reduces this part of the taxable gain to 7/9th x £12,000 x 25% = £2,333.

During the period 6 April 1998 to 5 April 2000 the shares counted as non-business assets. Non-business taper relief reduces this part of the gain to

2/9th x £12,000 x 65% = £1,733. Bella's taxable gain after taper relief is £2,333 + £1,733 = £4,066.

Bella's husband, Richard, also has a 3 per cent holding in Hammerson Ltd. They look at whether it would be more tax-efficient if Richard instead of Bella gave shares to Phoebe.

Richard first acquired his shares on 6 April 2000. Coincidentally, on 10 May 2007, Richard would also have a gain of £12,000 if he gave away the shares. The shares count as a business asset throughout the seven complete years that Richard has held them and so qualify for 75 per cent taper relief. This reduces Richard's taxable gain to £12,000 x 25% = £3,000.

Even though Richard has not held Hammerson shares for as long as Bella, his taxable gain is significantly lower (£3,000 compared with Bella's £4,066). It would, therefore, be more tax-efficient for Richard to make the gift to Phoebe.

63

INHERITANCE TAX AND BUSINESS ASSETS

Business assets may also qualify for extra IHT relief. If you give away something that counts as business property and you have owned it for at least two years immediately prior to making the gift, you can claim a 100 per cent relief to eliminate your IHT bill – this is called business property relief.

The definition of business property includes holdings of unquoted shares of eligible companies, including those traded on AIM. Relief does not apply to companies that are wholly or mainly engaged in dealing in shares or securities, dealing in land or buildings, or making and holding investments. Unlike the CGT rules, the definition of business property does not include furnished holiday lettings.

A gift of business property might count as a PET and become taxable if you die within seven years. Business property relief can then be claimed, provided:

- The recipient still owns the asset, or
- The recipient no longer owns it but has fully reinvested the proceeds in other assets that also qualify for business property relief.

❝Business assets may qualify for extra IHT relief. The definition of business property includes holdings of unquoted shares of eligible companies, including those traded on AIM. ❞

If you are planning to give away your business, you should seek advice from an accountant and solicitor.

64

Lifetime gifts with strings attached

It could be useful to make a gift but keep some rights to use it yourself. This is unlikely to save you IHT and could even land you with a yearly income tax bill. In addition, you might want to make a gift but put some conditions on how it is used. Trusts let you do just that and can still be set up efficiently despite recent changes to the way trusts are taxed.

4

Gifts you can still use

Most gifts of this sort can't save your estate IHT and might even trigger an income tax bill in your lifetime. But there are some exceptions.

GIFTS WITH RESERVATION

Problems can arise if you give something away but continue to benefit from it in some way. Special IHT rules (see opposite) apply to gifts like these:

- **The person receiving the gift does not really take possession of it**. For example, you might give a valuable painting to someone but carry on hanging it in your home.

> **!** The gift-with-reservation rules have no impact on capital gains tax (CGT). For CGT purposes, your gift is effective at the time you make it, even if it is a gift with reservation for IHT. The gifted asset is not part of your estate at death for CGT purposes, so the exemption from CGT at death cannot apply. Any increase in the value of the asset between the time you gave it away and the time you die is a capital gain built up in the hands of the recipient and tax may be due when he or she eventually disposes of the asset.

❝ Problems can arise if you give something away but continue to benefit from it. ❞

- **You carry on deriving some benefit** from the thing you give away unless you pay a full market rate – or the equivalent in kind – for your use of the asset. This might happen if, for example, you give your home to your children but you retain the right to live in all or part of the property rent-free.

These are 'gifts with reservation'. A gift with reservation still counts as part of your estate when you die and so does not escape IHT. A gift can stop being a gift with reservation if your use or benefit stops and you survive seven years after that. A gift might not be a gift with reservation at the time you make it, but can become one later on if you subsequently start to use it or benefit from it. For example, suppose you give someone a painting that continues to hang in your house but pay a full commercial rent to the owner for your use of the picture, this would take the gift outside the gift-with-reservation rules. But if the rent is not reviewed and, after say five years, it ceases to be a commercial amount, at that stage, the gift would become a gift with reservation and the painting would once more form part of your estate for IHT purposes.

66

How a gift with reservation is taxed

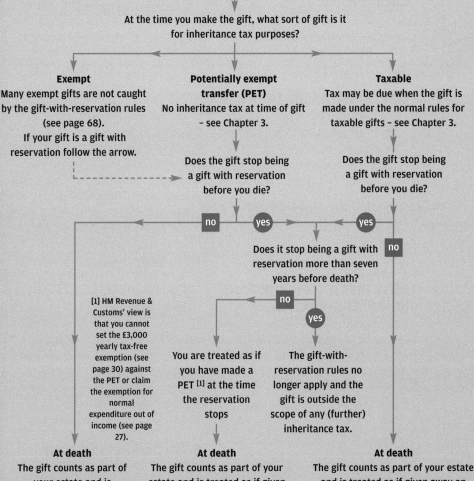

START

At the time you make the gift, what sort of gift is it for inheritance tax purposes?

Exempt
Many exempt gifts are not caught by the gift-with-reservation rules (see page 68).
If your gift is a gift with reservation follow the arrow.

Potentially exempt transfer (PET)
No inheritance tax at time of gift – see Chapter 3.

Does the gift stop being a gift with reservation before you die?

Taxable
Tax may be due when the gift is made under the normal rules for taxable gifts – see Chapter 3.

Does the gift stop being a gift with reservation before you die?

no   yes   yes

Does it stop being a gift with reservation more than seven years before death?   no

[1] HM Revenue & Customs' view is that you cannot set the £3,000 yearly tax-free exemption (see page 30) against the PET or claim the exemption for normal expenditure out of income (see page 27).

no

yes

You are treated as if you have made a PET [1] at the time the reservation stops

The gift-with-reservation rules no longer apply and the gift is outside the scope of any (further) inheritance tax.

At death
The gift counts as part of your estate and is treated as if given away on death. Normal rules for gifts from the estate apply – see Chapter 9.

At death
The gift counts as part of your estate and is treated as if given away on death. Normal rules for gifts from the estate apply – see Chapter 9. But tax may also be due on the PET in the normal way (see page 57). If so, special rules apply to stop the gift being taxed twice. If the original gift was taxed, credit is given for tax already paid.

At death
The gift counts as part of your estate and is treated as if given away on death. Normal rules for gifts from the estate apply – see Chapter 9. But credit is given for tax already paid when the gift was originally made.
If death is within seven years of making the original gift, extra tax may also be due on the gift in the normal way (see page 52). If so, special rules apply to stop the gift being taxed twice.

67

GIFTS THAT ARE NOT CAUGHT

Some gifts with strings attached are not caught by the gift-with-reservation rules and so are effective in reducing your estate for IHT purposes.

Gifts made a long time ago

The gift-with-reservation rules do not apply to any gifts made before 18 March 1986.

« There is no gift with reservation if your husband, wife or civil partner rather than you benefits. »

Gifts that are exempt from inheritance tax

If the original gift is covered by certain of the exemptions outlined in Chapter 2, the gift-with-reservation rules do not apply. The exemptions are:

- Gifts between husband and wife and, from 5 December 2005 onwards, gifts between civil partners (but see below)
- Gifts to charities and certain other bodies
- Gifts of national heritage property
- Gifts to political parties
- Gifts to housing associations
- Small gifts (up to £250 per person)
- Wedding gifts.

Note that the above list does not include all types of exempt lifetime gift. In particular, the gift-with-reservation rules can apply even though a gift is exempt at the time it is made because it is 'normal expenditure out of income' or covered by the £3,000 yearly tax-free exemption.

For gifts made from 20 June 2003 onwards, the law was changed so that the gift-with-reservation rules do apply to gifts between husbands and wives or gifts between civil partners in the following circumstances:

- The gifted asset(s) are put into a trust giving your spouse or civil partner an interest in possession.
- The interest in possession later ends before the giver's death, and
- The spouse or partner then neither becomes the outright owner of the property nor gets a further interest in possession in it.

These 2003 rules were introduced specifically to stop complex tax avoidance arrangements known as 'Eversden schemes'. For general information about trusts and what an 'interest in possession' is, see page 77 onwards.

Gifts that benefit your spouse or civil partner

There is no gift with reservation if your husband, wife or civil partner rather than you uses or benefits from the item you give away. But you must make sure there is no way in which you could potentially benefit. For example, if it is a gift of money, it should not be paid into an account that your spouse or civil partner holds jointly with you.

68

Gifts you pay to use

A gift of land or chattels is not a gift with reservation if you pay the full market rent (or full payment in kind) for using it or benefiting from it. For example, you might give a son or daughter a piece of furniture but continue to keep it at your home. If you pay to insure it and pay your child an appropriate rent based on an independent, professional valuation of the item, you should normally be outside the gift-with-reservation rules.

Gifts you share without benefiting by more than your share

Without triggering the gift-with-reservation rules, you are allowed to give away part of land or property – for example, your home – and share it with the co-owner(s), provided you do not benefit in any way from the bit you've given away. For example, you would have to bear your full share of the bills. See Chapter 10 for more information.

Gifts that are separated from the part you keep

If you can carve up a possession which you intend to give away and keep a distinct part of it that forms a separate asset in its own right (a process called 'shearing'), you can give away the remainder without the part you retain counting as a gift with reservation.

However, these days you will be caught by the gift-with-reservation rules if you apply shearing to gifts of land or property by, for example, splitting your ownership into a lease that you keep and a freehold that you sell (called a lease-carve-out or 'Ingram scheme'). This is because of anti-avoidance rules that came into effect in 1999. Ingram schemes set up before 9 March 1999 continue successfully to fall outside the gift-with-reservation rules.

Case Study | Sybil

Sybil invests a lump sum in a school fees plan designed to pay fees for her grandson, Harry. The arrangement allows for the policy to return a lump sum to Sybil if Harry were to die before finishing his education at the school. The payment of school fees is the gift from Sybil to Harry and the right to the refund is not deemed to be part of the gift (and is essentially a separate asset that Sybil keeps), so there is no gift with reservation.

See page 77 onwards for information about trusts. See Chapter 10 for things to consider if giving away or sharing your home.

69

Reservation of benefit due to infirmity

The gift-with-reservation rules will not apply if the benefit or use you derive from land you gave away has arisen because of unforeseen changes that mean you can no longer take care of yourself because of old age, illness or disability. This could apply if, say, you give the family home to your children and move out – perhaps to somewhere smaller and more manageable. If later, you have to move in with the children so they can care for you, this will not trigger the gift-with-reservation rules. For this exception to apply, the person who receives the gift must be a relative of you or your husband, wife or civil partner.

PRE-OWNED ASSETS TAX

Tax advisers are clever people and, over the years, a variety of schemes have grown up to get around the gift-with-reservation rules. Two – Ingram schemes and Eversden schemes – have been briefly mentioned earlier in this chapter. For many years, these and other avoidance schemes were typically used only by people with fairly substantial wealth. But, as rising house prices during the 1990s and 2000s have brought many 'ordinary' people potentially into the IHT net, some schemes started to be marketed more widely.

HM Revenue & Customs typically countered each avoidance scheme as it arose with challenges in the courts and changes to the law. But generally each Revenue success in stopping future use of a scheme has left a trail of successful tax avoiders who had bolted before the stable door was closed. The Revenue decided on a new tack and, from April 2005 onwards, introduced the pre-owned assets tax (POAT).

What is POAT?

POAT is a yearly income tax charge on the benefit you are deemed to get from something you used to own, or provided the money for, for example if you sell your home to your children but carry on living there, or you give them cash to

> ## "The scope for complicated lifetime IHT planning is now severely restricted. "

See page 77 onwards for information about trusts generally. See page 93 for trusts for children.

buy a home and then they let you move in. 'Benefit' includes, for example, occupying land, using an asset or receiving income from it. POAT is mainly aimed at gifts that escape the IHT gift-with-reservation rules, but its scope is much wider.

A tax with a past

POAT is an extremely unusual tax for two reasons:

- **It is an income tax** being used to plug loopholes in a completely different tax, namely IHT.
- **It is 'retroactive'.** The government points out that POAT does not go back and reassess you for tax for previous years and, on that basis, insists that this is not a 'retrospective' tax. But the

> **!** The government has warned that it is prepared to make further use of retroactive legislation so that actions you take now that successfully save tax cease to be effective once the law is changed. This means that the scope for complicated lifetime IHT planning is now severely restricted because any scheme that is successful in saving IHT on your estate is likely to draw HMRC's attention and may result in some other compensating tax charge.

Jargon buster

Arm's length The term HM Revenue & Customs use to describe the sort of commercial deal you would make with someone you did not know on the open market as opposed to a special arrangement you might strike with a friend or family member

Intangible asset Something you own that has no physical presence, such as cash, shares, insurance policies or other financial assets. You may be caught by POAT if you put cash, insurance policies or other intangible assets into a trust where, under income tax rules, any income from the trust is taxed as if it is yours. Under the POAT rules, 'trust' does not include a 'bare trust' (see page 79). You are not caught if the trust benefits your husband, wife or civil partner but not you

point is debatable. New tax measures normally apply only to actions taken on or after the date the measures come into effect. By contrast, POAT can impose a tax charge now on actions you took in the past.

Who has to pay POAT?

Three types of assets are affected: land (meaning buildings as well as just land), chattels (for example furniture, paintings, jewellery, books) and **intangible assets**. In the case of land or chattels, POAT may affect you if you can benefit from:

71

- An asset you have disposed of at any time on or after 18 March 1986 (called the 'disposal condition'), or
- An asset owned by someone to whom you have given money within the last seven years in order to directly or indirectly fund their acquiring the asset (called the 'contribution condition').

POAT does not just apply to gifts but other types of disposal too, such as sales.

There are a number of exemptions from POAT – see the table opposite. In addition, POAT does not apply if the person who made the gift and receives the benefit is not resident in the UK. If you are resident in the UK but your domicile (the place you consider to be your permanent home) is elsewhere, POAT can apply only to assets you have in the UK not elsewhere in the world.

Planning point

You are not caught by the POAT contribution condition if you only acted as guarantor for a loan taken out by someone else.

❝ POAT does not just apply to gifts but other types of disposal too, such as sales. ❞

Case Study Jack and Angela

Jack and Angela sold the family home to their daughter, Lizzie, and her husband, at a knock-down price and bought themselves a bungalow. After Jack died, Angela's health deteriorated and now she can no longer cope on her own. She moves back into the family home so that Lizzie can look after her. Although Angela is now using the home she sold at less than its full value, this is caught by neither the IHT gift-with-reservation rules nor POAT because the reason for her use was unforeseen and due to her old age and ill health.

For answers to frequently asked questions about POAT, see the HM Revenue & Customs website at www.hmrc.gov.uk/poa/poa_faqs.htm.

72

Transactions to which POAT does not apply

A transaction involving:	Is not caught by POAT if:
Land, possessions or intangible assets	The yearly benefit from all your transactions caught by POAT, before deducting anything you pay the owner(s), comes to no more than £5,000. (If it exceeds £5,000, the whole amount not just the excess is taxable.)
	The asset is still part of your estate for IHT.
	It is a gift with reservation for IHT.
	It is a gift where you have opted to be treated as if it were a gift with reservation (see page 75).
	It is a gift exempt from IHT and also the gift-with-reservation rules (see page 68).
	You pay full market rent for your benefit.
	You share the asset and benefit no more than your fair share.
Land or possessions	You disposed of the whole asset at **arm's length** or on arm's length terms. You can retain rights for yourself if they can be carved out as a separate asset in the same way as applies under the gift-with-reservation rules (see page 69).
	You disposed of part of the asset at arm's length to someone not connected with you. [1] This exempts, for example, an equity release scheme (see page 184) where you sell part of your home to a commercial company.
	You disposed of part of the asset to someone who is connected with you [1] on arm's length terms, but only if the transaction took place before 7 March 2005. This exemption could cover an informal equity release scheme where you had sold part of your home to a relative in return for cash or income.
	You disposed of part of the asset on arm's length terms on or after 7 March 2005 where the amount paid to you is not in cash or assets readily convertible to cash. This could cover a situation where you gave part of your home to someone who had moved in to be your carer in recognition of their caring services to you.
	It is a transfer to your husband, wife or civil partner or to a trust giving them an interest in possession (see page 80) for life.
	It is a transfer under a court order to a former husband, wife or civil partner or to a trust giving them an interest in possession (see page 80) for life.
	The reason for the disposal is the maintenance of your family.
	The disposal is an outright gift covered by the IHT-free yearly allowance (see page 30) or the small gifts exemption (see page 30).
	It is an outright cash gift used to buy land or possessions where the gift was made more than at least seven years before you started to benefit from the asset.
	Your use of the land started only because you were no longer able to care for yourself because of old age or infirmity.

[1] For the purpose of POAT, a 'connected person' includes your husband, wife, civil partner, child, brother, sister, grandparent (and their parents, grandparents and so on), grandchild (and their children and so on down the line), uncles, aunts, nieces, nephews and trusts of which you are the settlor.

73

How POAT works

The benefit you are deemed to receive from an asset you have given away or contributed towards is added to your other income for the year and income tax is charged in the normal way.

POAT works in a similar way to income tax on the value of fringe benefits you get through a job. The benefit you are deemed to get depends on the type of asset:

- **Land**. The full market rent you would otherwise have to pay. If you benefit from only part of the property, the benefit is a proportion of the full market rent. You can deduct any rent you actually pay to the owner.
- **Chattels**. The market value of the asset multiplied by an official interest rate set by HM Revenue & Customs (used also in connection with valuing loans from employers to employees). The interest rate is usually set for a year at a time and in 2006–7 was 5 per cent. For example, if the item was valued at £50,000, the yearly benefit would be 5% x £50,000 = £2,500. The benefit is scaled down if you use only part of the possession and you can deduct any amount you actually pay the owner for your use of the asset.
- **Intangible property**. The market value of the trust property multiplied by the official interest rate (5 per cent in 2006–7) less any income tax or CGT you already pay on the property.

The value of an asset is generally the value it could be expected to fetch if sold on the open market. Assets must be valued on the first day of the tax year (6 April) or, if later, the date the asset first came within the POAT regime. Land and possessions are valued only once every five years with each valuation applying unchanged for the whole five year period.

Planning point

Where a land valuation takes place at a time when asset prices are low, the POAT charge for the next five years is also low, but there could be a large jump at the next valuation if asset prices are then much higher.

 To check the current official rate of interest, see the HM Revenue & Customs website, www.hmrc.gov.uk/rates/interest-beneficial.htm. Valuing the benefit from intangible property is a complex area. Contact any adviser who set up or helps you run the trust for further information.

Your options under POAT

If you have a transaction that is caught by POAT, you have four options:

- **Pay the yearly POAT charge.** POAT is a charge on benefit you are deemed to get not actual income, so to pay POAT you will need to have income or other resources you can dip into.
- **Pay the full market rent** to the owner of the asset for your use of it. Again, you need to have enough income or other resources to afford this option.
- **Unscramble the transaction** so that it returns to your estate or becomes subject to the IHT gift-with-reservation rules. No POAT is due, but IHT may be payable on the asset when you die. Unscrambling might not be possible. Under the transaction, legal ownership has normally passed to someone else. They may be unwilling or unable to give the property back. In addition, unscrambling may incur costs and CGT charges.
- **Without unscrambling the transaction, opt to be treated as if the inheritance tax gift-with-reservation rules apply.** This means no POAT is payable but IHT may be due when you die. You have until 31 January following the end of the tax year in which you first became subject to POAT to make this election. But, following a Budget 2007 change, the Revenue can accept a late election. Once the election is made, the election is irreversible, so you can't change your mind later on and decide you would

rather the gift-with-reservation rules didn't apply after all.

Electing to be treated as if the gift-with-reservation rules apply affects only the IHT position. For CGT, you continue to have disposed of the asset on the date the transaction took place. Any increase in the value of the asset between then and the date of death accrues in the hands of the new owner and may be liable to CGT when they dispose of the asset. By contrast, if the asset had been part of your estate, any taxable gain would have been wiped out by the exemption from CGT for assets given away on death.

Planning point

If the benefits you get from all the assets caught by POAT come to no more than £5,000, there is no POAT to pay. In that case, you might decide to stay within the POAT regime, but consider how the value of the asset concerned might change in future.

Paying the owner a full market rent could be a good option if you can afford it and you would, in any case, like to pass on more of your wealth to the owner. For example, you might have given your home to your children under a scheme that got around the gift-with-reservation rules and you can now pass them a regular sum each year in the form of rent. However, the rent will count as taxable income in the hands of your children.

Coming back within the gift-with-reservation rules (either by unscrambling or election) would not cause an IHT problem if your estate at death would in any case be less than the tax-free slice (£300,000 in 2007-8).

75

Case Study Molly

Molly, like many pensioners, is 'cash-poor, asset-rich'. She struggles to manage on her pensions but lives in a valuable home. She has been thinking about taking out a home reversion scheme (see Chapter 10), whereby she would sell part of her home to a company for a lump sum but retain the right to live in the home until she dies (or, if necessary, moves permanently into care).

Her grandson, Dan, suggests that instead of going to a reversion company, he could buy a share of her home and give her a better deal than a company. If Molly and Dan had made such an arrangement before 7 March 2005, there would have been no problem. But, from that date onwards, such arrangements are caught by POAT and Molly will become liable to tax each year on her benefit from living in the part of the home she sells to Dan if it exceeds the £5,000 threshold at which POAT becomes due. They work out if this will be the case.

Molly's home is worth £300,000. Dan is willing to pay her the full £150,000 for a half share. A local estate agent advises that the rent they could charge if they let out the home would be £450 a month. This comes to £5,400 a year and so Molly's benefit from using the half the home that was sold would be 50% x £5,400 = £2,700. This is less than the POAT threshold, so Dan and Molly decide to go ahead with the scheme.

Telling the taxman

It's up to you to realise if you are caught by POAT and you must declare any liability on your tax return. If you do not receive a tax return, tell your tax office by 5 October following the end of the tax year in which the liability started and you will be sent a form.

If you want to opt out of POAT by electing to be treated as if the gift-with-reservation rules apply, use form IHT500 available from HM Revenue & Customs and send it in no later then 31 January following the year in which the liability to POAT starts. For example, if you started to be liable for POAT in 2007–8, you must make the election by 31 January 2009.

❝ It's up to you to realise if you are caught by POAT and you must declare any liability on your tax return. ❞

Gifts using trusts

You can retain some flexibility about who benefits from your gifts and how they are used by setting up trusts.

Trusts let you give away assets but retain some control over how they are used. They are also frequently used as a way of reducing IHT that might otherwise be payable on death. Trusts can be set up during your lifetime or under a will.

" Trusts let you give away assets but retain some control. "

Jargon buster

Settlement Term used in tax legislation to mean most arrangements or agreements that transfers assets with some element of 'bounty' (meaning some element of gift to the recipient). Trusts are sometimes referred to as settlements but 'settlement' includes many other types of arrangement as well

WHAT IS A TRUST?

A trust is an arrangement where the legal owners of assets (which can be things like money, land, buildings and so on) hold the assets and must use them for the benefit of someone else. There are three conditions that must be met for the creation of a trust:

- The intention to create it must be clear from the words used.
- The trust property must be identified.
- It must be clear who is to benefit from the trust.

(In Scotland, there is a further requirement that trust assets or evidence of their ownership is physically delivered to the trustees or, alternatively, that the trust is registered in the Books of Council and Session.)

It is usual to set out this information and other conditions in a written deed, but trusts can come into being without anything being put into writing.

 Trusts are complex and need to be drawn up by a solicitor (or insurance company, which will use its own solicitors) – see page 82.

77

❝ Perhaps you're not sure at this stage who should benefit from your gift or you want to be able to change who benefits or the amount they get. ❞

Who's involved in a trust?

- **The settlor** (called the truster or granter in Scotland). This is the person who gives away the assets to be placed in the trust. A trust may have more than one settlor and this does not have to be an individual. For example, the settlor could be a company or another trust.
- **The trustees.** There is usually more than one trustee and these are the legal owners of the trust property. So the property is registered in their names, and they are responsible for holding it safely and accounting for it. The settlor can be a trustee, so too can a beneficiary.
- **The beneficiaries.** There might be one beneficiary or more. These are the people who will – or might – share the trust property and any income from it. Beneficiaries can be individuals, companies, charities or other bodies. Different beneficiaries may have different rights. The settlor can be a beneficiary of the trust, but this has tax implications – see page 88.

WHY USE TRUSTS?

Trusts can be useful in many situations, for example:

- **Giving to children.** You might want to make a gift now to a child to be available to him or her later, for example, when they reach an age you specify.
- **Maintaining control.** The person you want to benefit might not be good at handling money. For example, they have learning difficulties or a tendency to be a spendthrift.
- **Giving to a group.** Maybe you want to give to a group of people that is not yet complete – for example, your grandchildren including those yet to be born.
- **Retaining flexibility.** Perhaps you're not sure at this stage who should benefit from your gift or you want to be able to change who benefits or the amount they get if circumstances change. Provided you specify the range of potential beneficiaries now, you can leave these decisions until later.
- **Separating income from capital.** This lets you specify that someone will have your assets in the end but, in the meantime, someone else has the income from them or the use of them. This can be particularly useful in family situations – for example, if you want a widow or widower to be financially secure but ultimately want your children (maybe from a former marriage) to benefit.
- **Giving on special occasions or in set circumstances.** You might want to

make a gift only on the occasion of some possible but indeterminate event, such as a marriage or birth. Similarly, you might want someone to benefit now but for your gift to pass to someone else if, say, the first beneficiary goes bankrupt.

- **Maintaining confidentiality.** A beneficiary does not have to know that you have arranged a gift to be made at some future time. Similarly, a beneficiary in receipt of income or capital from a trust does not have to know who the settlor was.
- **Tax-efficiency.** Sometimes a gift into trust can save you tax, or avoid tax problems that would arise with an outright gift. But the scope for saving tax has been reduced by changes in the 2006 Finance Act (see page 82).

THE MAIN TYPES OF TRUST

There are three main types of trust. Which is suitable for your needs depends on what you are trying to achieve.

Bare trust

How does it work? This is a very simple type of trust. Someone holds assets as nominee for someone else – for example, a parent holds investments for their child. Once the beneficiary is aged 18 or more (or is married if younger), he or she can call for the income and/or capital at any time and the trustee has no right to withhold it. For tax purposes, the beneficiary – not the trustee – is treated as the owner of the trust property.

A bare trust is easy to set up and administer. But watch out if you are a

parent making a gift to your child to be held in a bare trust as any income may be taxed as yours not the child's – see Chapter 5. Income from gifts from other sources – for example, from grandparents – and any capital gains count as those of the child. This can make a bare trust more tax-efficient than other trust options in suitable cases. Against this, you must balance the drawbacks. Once the trust is set up, you cannot change the beneficiaries or the shares in which they own the trust property. The settlor has no control at all over the use of the trust property once a child has reached their majority. The trust property is part of the beneficiary's estate when he or she dies – if the beneficiary is under the age of 18 (12 in Scotland) at the time of death, they would die intestate (see Chapter 8) since they would be too young to have made a will.

Possible uses

- Making a gift of property to a child – e.g. a share in a family business – which the child does not yet have the legal capacity to hold because of his or her young age.
- Building up a nest-egg for a child to have on reaching age 18. (But, for children born on or after 1 September 2002, consider also the child trust fund – see Chapter 5.)

❝ A bare trust is easy to set up and administer. ❞

Lifetime gifts with strings attached

79

Interest-in-possession trust

Also known as a 'life-interest trust' or 'fixed-interest trust'.

How does it work? One or more beneficiaries have the right to receive income earned by the assets in the trust as that income arises or they have the right to use the assets held by the trust, for example, the right to live in a house. This is called a 'life interest'. Eventually the assets in the trust are distributed. This might happen, for example, on the death of the life-interest beneficiary or at a specified date or when a specified event, such as marriage, occurs. The person or people who then receive the assets are said to hold the 'reversionary interest'. You could give the same person both interests (the life interest from one date and the reversionary interest from a later date).

Possible uses

- Where you eventually want to pass on assets to one or more people but need to provide for someone else in the interim.
- Where you do not want the beneficiary to have full control of the assets in the trust or you want to defer handing over control until a later date.

Case Study David

David's will stipulates that, on his death, a large part of his assets should be placed in trust. The trustees would invest the assets as they saw fit and the income from them (and use of his former share of the family home) should go to his wife during her lifetime. On his wife's death, the assets are to be shared equally between their three children. David has drawn up his will in this way, first, to guard against his widow being short of money during her lifetime and, secondly, to ensure that his children will eventually receive his assets even if his widow remarries.

❝One or more beneficiaries have the right to receive income or to use the assets. Eventually the assets are distributed.❞

See pages 84 and 87 for how interest-in-possession trusts are taxed.

80

Discretionary trust

How does it work? If a trust is not a bare trust or an interest-in-possession trust, it is by default a discretionary trust. A distinguishing feature is that generally income can be accumulated within the trust to be paid out later or at the discretion of the trustees. Usually there is more than one beneficiary. Often there will be a 'class' of beneficiaries, such as your children or your grandchildren, not all of whom have to be born at the time the trust is set up.

Possible uses
- Where you want the ability to alter who will benefit under the trust.
- Where you want to be able to alter the proportions in which the beneficiaries share in income and/or capital from the trust.

Case Study — John

John had been ill for some time and, knowing that he did not have long to live, he checked his will and brought it up to date. He was a widower with three adult sons. One had a good, secure income, another had not settled down to a career yet but had only minor financial problems, while the third son was generally in financial difficulties – largely of his own making. John wanted to be fair to all his boys but was not happy with the idea of just sharing out his assets between them. They did not all have the same need and the youngest son in particular would be likely to squander any inheritance. John decided to set up a discretionary trust in favour of all the sons. He appointed his own two brothers (the sons' uncles) as trustees and gave them discretion to make payments and loans from the trust fund to the sons if or when, in the trustees' opinion, such help was warranted. After ten years (by which time John felt the boys should all take responsibility for themselves), the remaining trust assets were to be distributed equally among them.

❝ Income in a discretionary trust can generally be accumulated to be paid out later at the discretion of the trustees. ❞

Accumulation-and-maintenance trust

This is a type of discretionary trust to benefit children. Such trusts have been popular in the past because they received favourable IHT treatment. This treatment no longer applies to trusts set up on or after 22 March 2006 which are now taxed in the same way as other discretionary trusts. There are transitional tax rules (see page 94) for accumulation-and-maintenance trusts set up before that date.

81

SETTING UP A TRUST

A bare trust can be set up very easily – for example, by simply stating on an application form that you are holding savings or investments on behalf of someone else.

With other trusts, it is best to use a formal, written deed that makes your intentions crystal clear. Get professional help setting up a trust from a solicitor either direct or through an accountant, tax adviser or independent financial adviser (IFA). Depending on the complexity of the trust and the value of the assets concerned, creating a trust can be expensive (costing hundreds, even thousands, of pounds), so check that the benefits warrant the financial outlay.

Life insurance products are very often used in conjunction with trusts. Many life insurance companies can provide you with off-the-peg trust documents that let you very simply, and usually at no extra cost, opt to have a life policy written in trust. You can either arrange this direct with the insurance company or through an IFA.

HOW TRUSTS ARE TAXED

The 2006 Finance Act made major changes to IHT on trusts. Virtually all trusts are now taxed under the regime, which previously applied only to discretionary trusts (see page 84). For exceptions, see page 87. Trusts are also subject to income tax and CGT. Bare trusts fall outside the tax regime that applies to more complex trusts.

Case Study Seb

Seb is the beneficiary of a bare trust containing £10,000 capital. This was a gift from his grandmother. The capital has earned approximately £400 a year income and some small capital gains. Both are well within Seb's income tax allowance CGT allowances. On reaching 18, Seb intends to ask the trustee, his dad, to carry on acting as trustee but to advance Seb regular sums to support him while at university. On finishing university, Seb intends to take outright possession of the remaining trust property (if any). As he is already treated as the outright owner, no transfer takes place and so there will be no IHT.

“ Creating a trust can be expensive (costing hundreds, even thousands, of pounds), so check that the benefits warrant the financial outlay. ”

The taxation of trusts is complicated. Get advice from the firm you are using to set up your trust.

82

Bare trusts

Putting a gift into trust	Unless you can use one of the exemptions described in Chapter 2, your gift into a bare trust normally counts as a PET (see Chapter 3) [1], so there is no IHT to pay provided you survive for at least seven years. No special rules apply regarding CGT – check the ordinary rules in Chapter 3 to see if any CGT will be payable on the gift.
The trust's tax position	Income and gains from the trust property are treated in the same way as if the property was owned directly by the beneficiary. This means that income is taxed at the beneficiary's top rate after taking into account allowances and any other deductions. The exception to this is where the assets in the trust are a gift from a parent to a child, in which case income may be taxed as that of the parent – see Chapter 5. Gains are taxed at the beneficiary's top rate after taking account of the yearly tax-free allowance.
Payments to beneficiaries	Where, as is usual, tax has already been paid as income and gains arose, there is no further tax to pay when payments are made to the beneficiary or used for his or her benefit. But see Chapter 5 regarding gifts from a parent.
When the bare trust ends	The trust property has been treated as owned by the beneficiary throughout. Therefore there is no change when the beneficiary takes outright possession of the trust property.

[1] In early 2007, HMRC had suggested that, as a (probably unintentional) result of the Finance Act 2006 changes, the IHT treatment of a gift to a bare trust depended on the age of the recipient. If the recipient is under age 18 (or 16 in Scotland), because the child has no access to income from the trust, the trust should be taxed like a discretionary trust (see overleaf). If the recipient is over age 18 (16), the recipient would have an immediate right to income, making the gift akin to an outright gift and so treated as a PET for IHT purposes. At the time of writing, HMRC was considering the position and clarification was awaited.

83

Most other trusts set up on or after 22 March 2006

Putting a gift into trust	This is a taxable gift for IHT, unless you can claim one of the exemptions in Chapter 2. So the gift can create an immediate tax bill (see Chapter 3), unless when added to other taxable gifts you have made within the last seven years, it is within your tax-free limit (£300,000 in 2007–8). CGT may be due, if you are giving assets other than cash, but you can claim hold-over relief (see page 59).
The trust's inheritance tax position	There is a 'periodic charge' on the value of the trust property. This is made on each tenth anniversary of the setting-up of the trust. Tax due is worked out as shown in the calculator overleaf. If money or assets are paid out of the trust, an exit charge must be paid by the trustees. The charge is worked out by multiplying the full ten-year charge by 1/40 for each three-month period during which the property was in the trust since the last periodic charge. The tax charge is scaled down similarly if the property was added to the trust after the start of the relevant ten-year period.
The trust's income tax position: discretionary trusts	Tax on income is paid at the 'rate applicable to trusts' (RAT), which is 32.5 per cent on dividends and 40 per cent on other income. All trusts liable for the RAT on income benefit from a basic-rate band (£1,000 in 2007–8). Income falling within the basic rate band is taxed at 10 per cent (dividends), 20 per cent (savings income) or 22 per cent (other income).
The trust's income tax position: interest-in-possession trusts	Income from the assets in the trust may be paid either direct to the beneficiaries or first to the trustees who then pass it on to the beneficiaries. The trustees are responsible for tax at different rates depending on the type of income. The 2007–8 rates are 10 per cent on dividends, 20 per cent on savings income and 22 per cent on other income.
The trust's CGT position	CGT on any taxable capital gains is also payable by the trustees at the RAT of 40 per cent in 2007–8, though the trust can set a tax-free allowance (usually half the amount individuals get, so £4,600 in 2007–8) against the first slice of gains.

84

Income payments to beneficiaries: discretionary trusts	Income is all paid out with tax at a notional rate of 40 per cent already deducted. You receive the net income plus a 40 per cent tax credit. The sum of the two counts as your gross income against which you can set the tax credit. This means, unless you are a higher-rate taxpayer, you can claim a refund of part or all of the tax.
Income payments to beneficiaries: interest-in-possession trusts	Income paid out to beneficiaries is broadly treated as if it had been received directly by them. Three different treatments may apply, depending on the type of income: • Dividends are received net of tax at 10 per cent and accompanied by a tax credit. Non-taxpayers cannot reclaim this tax credit. Starting- and basic-rate taxpayers have no further tax to pay. Higher-rate taxpayers must pay further tax of 22.5 per cent on the grossed-up amount of the dividend. • Savings income is paid net of tax at 20 per cent. Non-taxpayers can reclaim this. Starting-rate taxpayers can reclaim half the tax deducted. Basic-rate taxpayers have no further tax to pay. Higher-rate taxpayers must pay extra tax of 20 per cent on the grossed-up amount of the interest. • Other income is paid with tax at the basic rate already deducted. Non-taxpayers can reclaim all the tax deducted and starting-rate taxpayers can reclaim 12 per cent. Higher-rate taxpayers have extra tax of 18 per cent to pay on the grossed-up income.
Capital payments to beneficiaries	If you receive a payment of capital from the trust, there is no CGT for you to pay and you cannot reclaim any CGT paid by the trust. Note that, once income has been accumulated within the trust, the payment of it to a beneficiary will normally count as a payment of capital.
When the trust ends	An IHT exit charge is made on the whole of the trust property as if it were any other payment from the trust (see above).

Calculator: working out the periodic charge

		Example (2007-8)
Value of trust at time of periodic charge	**A** £	A £310,000
Value of gifts in seven years up to the date the trust was set up	**B** £	B £90,000
Add A and B	**C** £	C £400,000
Tax-free limit for year of periodic charge	**D** £	D £300,000
C minus D	**E** £	E £100,000
Multiply E by lifetime IHT rate of 20%	**F** £	F £20,000
Divide F by A to find the effective rate of tax	**G** %	G 6.452%
Multiply G by 30%	**H** %	H 1.936%
Multiply H by A to find periodic charge now due	**I** £	I £6,001

Planning point

A reversionary interest in an interest-in-possession trust is treated as a separate asset from the interest in possession and counts as 'excluded property' outside the IHT net. This means the gift of a reversionary interest cannot create an IHT bill. There is no CGT either provided you are the beneficiary for whom the interest was created or, if not, you did not buy the interest.

Trusts that receive favourable inheritance tax treatment

The three types of trust opposite qualify for the following IHT treatment:

- **Putting the assets into trust.** This is not taxable.
- **The trust's tax position.** There are no periodic or exit charges.

The IHT rules for interest-in-possession trusts and accumulation-and-maintenance trusts changed dramatically from Budget Day 2006. But there are transitional rules for trusts set up before that date. See Chapter 5 for the rules applying to existing accumulation-and-maintenance trusts. For existing interest-in-possession trusts, talk to the firm that originally set up your trust or administers the trust for you.

86

Trusts with favourable inheritance tax treatment

Immediate post-death interest (IPDI) trust	This is an interest-in-possession trust that starts up on someone's death on or after 22 March 2006. It gives one or more people – for example, a surviving partner – a life interest. The person with the life interest is treated as if they own the assets outright. If the interest ends during their lifetime, the person with the life interest is treated as if they have made a PET to the recipient of the assets. If the interest ends on their death, the trust assets count as part of their estate and IHT may be due.
Bereaved minor's trust	A trust set up on the death of a parent to use assets from the parent for the benefit of their child (or children). For details, see Chapter 5.
Disabled person's trust	This is a trust set up either in life or in a will for the benefit of someone who has a permanent mental or physical incapacity – for example a trust set up by parents to provide lasting support for a disabled child. It can also be set up by someone with an existing health condition – for example, in the early stages of Alzheimer's disease – for their own benefit later on if they expect their condition to worsen. When the trust ends, IHT may be due on any remaining assets. In addition, the trustees and disabled person may jointly elect to have income and gains made by the trust treated as if they were received direct by the disabled person, so making use of their tax allowances and bands. The election must be made by 31 January falling one year and ten months after the first tax year from which the election is to apply (for example, by 31 January 2010 for the 2007–8 tax year). Once made the election cannot be reversed.

Settlor-interested trusts

A settlor-interested trust is one in which the settlor has a 'retained interest'. If this applies, both income and capital gains made by the trust will be taxed as those of the settlor. Often this will mean a higher tax bill.

You will be treated as having a retained interest if you or your husband, wife or civil partner can in any circumstances benefit from the trust either now or at some future time. From 6 April 2006, you will also be treated as having a retained interest if your dependent child or children can benefit from the trust.

The definition of retained interest is very wide, so you will be caught by the rules not simply if you or your husband, wife, civil partner or child is a named beneficiary of the trust, but even if you or they might become a beneficiary because of some seemingly unlikely circumstances, for example:

- The trust says your grandchild will become entitled to the trust property provided he or she reaches age 25 but you fail to say what happens if he or she does not reach that age. In that case, the property would automatically revert back to the settlor, so you are a potential beneficiary and have a retained interest.
- A trust is set up for grandchildren but the trustees have the power to give

the trust property to any other trust that includes the grandchildren as beneficiaries. This would not exclude a trust that also included you or your husband, wife, civil partner or child as additional beneficiaries, so again you are deemed to have a retained interest.

Note, too, that if you are both the settlor and an actual or potential beneficiary under the trust, the IHT gift-with-reservation rules apply (see page 66). The trust property will then continue to count as part of your estate. (Unlike the retained interest rules, the gift-with-reservation rules do not apply if your husband, wife, civil partner or dependent child is a beneficiary.) If you have an interest in the trust but have managed to set it up using a scheme that avoids the gift-with-reservation rules, the pre-owned assets tax (POAT) – see page 70 – might instead apply.

Most gifts to trusts are now taxable gifts for IHT, which generally opens the possibility of claiming hold-over relief from CGT (see page 59). But hold-over is not allowed where you make a gift to a settlor-interested trust.

For more information about CGT on settlor-interested trusts, see the free HM Revenue & Customs Helpsheet IR277 available from its Orderline 0845 9000 404 or downloadable from www.hmrc.gov.uk.

Giving to children

There are many reasons for wanting to make a gift to a child. You might want to build up a nest-egg that the child can draw on when, say, he or she goes to university or buys his or her first home. Alternatively, you might want the money to be available sooner to help with education costs or as a tool to help the child learn how to handle money.

How to organise your gift

There are two main concerns when considering gifts to children: the tax-avoidance rules that may affect gifts from a parent to a child, and how to arrange the gift, given that the child may be too young to hold an investment or to use the gift wisely.

GIFTS FROM PARENTS

Every person, however young, is within the tax system and so benefits from the basic tax allowances, in particular the personal allowance for income tax (£5,225 in 2007–8) and yearly tax-free slice for CGT (£9,200 in 2007–8).

In theory, families could save tax by spreading their income and assets across all family members including the children. But in the case of income tax, rules devised to stop tax avoidance prevent this.

The rules work like this. If a parent makes a gift to a child who is under the age of 18 and unmarried, and the gift produces more than £100 a year income, the whole of the income (not just the excess over £100) is taxed as that of the parent who made the gift.

The anti-avoidance rules do not apply to capital gains produced by a gift from a parent, nor do they apply to some types of tax-free income. So by choosing the investments carefully a parent can still make tax-efficient gifts to their child.

Investing for a tax-free income

If you invest a gift you have made to your own child and it produces tax-free income, in most cases the anti-avoidance rules do not apply so it will not matter if the gift produces more than £100 income. The exception here is cash individual savings accounts (ISAs).

Cash ISAs are not an option for most children because you have to be aged at least 16 to be eligible (and 18 for stocks and shares ISAs). There is no tax on income from an ISA so you might think

Planning point

The £100 limit applies to each parent and each child, so two parents could jointly make gifts to each child, which would produce up to £200 a year income without triggering the anti-avoidance rule.

 For more information on NS&I children's bonus bonds, see 'Investments for children' on page 96.

90

there would be no problem if parental gifts to a teenager were invested in cash ISAs. But, unusually for tax-free income, the anti-avoidance rules specifically apply to cash ISAs so, if the income from the parental gifts exceeded £100, it would be taxed as that of the parent.

The main investments that parents can make for their children without being taxed on the income are National Savings & Investments (NS&I) children's bonus bonds, friendly society tax-efficient savings plans, stakeholder pensions and the child trust fund.

Investing for gains instead of income

The £100 rule applies only to income from parental gifts, so you can get around it by giving your child investments that are expected to produce capital gains instead.

Suitable gifts might be growth-oriented unit trusts and open-ended investment companies (OEICs), and capital shares in split-capital investment trusts – see 'Investments for children' on page 96 for details. You could also consider collectors' items, such as paintings and antiques.

Gifts from other people

The £100 rule applies only to parental gifts. It does not affect gifts from grandparents, uncles, aunts, friends of the family or anyone else.

To avoid confusion with HM Revenue & Customs you should be able to distinguish these gifts from any parental gifts. It would be sensible to invest the

two types of gifts separately – for example, you could put small parental gifts in a building society account and gifts from other people in another account. It is also a good idea to ask people who give money to your child to accompany it with a brief note stating the amount of the gift and who it is from. Keep such notes and letters in a safe place in case HM Revenue & Customs need to see them.

Where a child is young, money is often given to the parents to invest or use on the child's behalf rather than being given directly to the child. This may in effect create a bare trust (see pages 79 and 83) with the parent as the trustee who must use the money as instructed by the person who made the gift. Even though the parent may then open an investment in the child's name, the gift should not count as a parental gift and so should not be caught by the anti-avoidance rules.

❝ Ask people who give money to your child to accompany it with a brief note. Keep such notes and letters in a safe place in case HMRC need to see them. ❞

91

THE TYPE OF GIFT

Before deciding which investments to choose for a child, you first need to decide how to arrange your gift.

Outright gift now

The most tax-efficient option is usually to make an immediate gift to the child. Often this means asking the child's parents (if you are not yourself the parent) to manage the investment on his or her behalf, but children can operate their own bank and building society accounts and NS&I investment accounts. They can also hold tax-efficient friendly society plans in their own names.

Earmarking your own savings to give later

You could invest money now in your own name and later on give the proceeds to the child. If you are not already making full use of your yearly ISA allowance, you could use this to invest for a tax-free return.

This option has the advantage of flexibility because you choose the precise timing of the gift and in the meantime you have the freedom to change your mind, for example, if you run short of money or the child turns out to be a spendthrift.

The main drawback is the failure to make use of the child's own tax allowances. In addition, the investment remains part of your estate until the gift is finally made. So if you die before handing over the gift, there could be IHT to pay.

Giving to a trust

Instead of making a gift direct to a child, you could put it in trust.

The simplest option is a bare trust (see page 79). If you hold something on bare trust for, say, your grandchild, the child is treated as the owner of the asset for tax purposes (but see footnote on page 83 regarding uncertainty over the IHT position), but he or she can also take possession as soon as he or she reaches age 18 (or marries if younger). This is also a drawback with the child trust fund, where the child can use the money from

Case Study Yuen

Yuen's granddaughter, Lily, has just started secondary school and Yuen wants to invest a lump sum of £3,000 to build up a nest-egg to help her when she reaches adulthood. The gift falls within Yuen's yearly tax-free allowance for IHT. He decides to put the money into a unit trust. Yuen is the legal owner of the units but the account is designated as 'Yuen Chan a/c Lily Chan'. This effectively creates a bare trust with Yuen holding the units as nominee for Lily. For tax purposes, Lily is the recipient of any income and gains from the units, and can set her allowances against them. To make doubly sure the bare trust is recognised, Yuen could write to his tax office saying that he has made this investment on behalf of Lily.

the fund in any way they like once they reach age 18.

Using a more formal trust – such as a discretionary trust (see Chapter 4) – gives you more control over the gift. Because of the costs of setting up such trusts, this will be appropriate only if you are giving a relatively large sum (say, £50,000 or more). A big advantage of a discretionary trust is flexibility – for example, you could set one up to benefit all your grandchildren, even those who are not yet born, and you can specify when the children will have access to the gift (or a share of it).

A special type of discretionary trust, called an 'accumulation-and-maintenance trust', has been popular in the past as a way of giving to children, because it benefited from special IHT advantages. But the IHT treatment of these trusts has changed from 22 March 2006 onwards. See pages 94 to 95 for details of how these trusts are taxed now.

USING TRUSTS

In the past, a popular route for making gifts to children has been an accumulation-and-maintenance trust. This was a discretionary trust (see page 81) that benefited from special IHT treatment:

- Gifts into the trust counted as PETs, so there was no IHT at the time of the gift and none at all if the giver survived seven years.
- No periodic (ten-year) or exit charges.

To qualify for this beneficial treatment, the trust had to comply with various rules, in particular one or more of the beneficiaries had to be entitled to income or capital from the trust by age 25. However, the Finance Act 2006 has swept away this beneficial tax treatment, with the exception of a new 'bereaved minor's trust'. There are transitional rules for accumulation-and-maintenance trusts set up before 22 March 2006.

❝ Using a more formal trust, such as a discretionary trust, gives you more control over the gift. ❞

> **!** If a living parent gives assets to a trust (other than a bare trust) that can benefit their dependent children, this counts as a 'settlor-interested trust' (see page 88). This means that capital gains made by the trust are taxed as gains of the parent rather than the trust and any income paid out to the child is taxed as income of the parent.

 At the time of writing, there was uncertainty about the IHT treatment of bare trusts for children. To check the current position, call the HM Revenue & Customs Inheritance Tax and Probate Helpline on 0845 302 0900.

Bereaved minor's trust

This is a trust set up either in your will or under the intestacy rules (see Chapter 8) so that your dependent child can benefit from assets left by you in the event of your death. The assets can only come from a dead parent's estate – for example, this can't be a trust set up by a grandparent to benefit an orphaned grandchild.

Provided the child takes over the trust assets completely by age 18, there is no IHT when the assets pass into the trust and no periodic or exit charge.

You might be reluctant to think of your child coming into a lot of money at age 18, when perhaps they might not be ready to use money wisely. The trust can be set up to delay that time as late as age 25, but then there will be IHT on the trust assets for the period from age 18 to 25 – see the box, opposite.

Planning point

If you have young children, consider changing your will to set up a bereaved minor's trust. This can be a tax efficient way to help make sure your children would be financially provided for in the event of your death.

New accumulation-and-maintenance trusts

Trusts set up on or after 22 March 2006 are taxed in the same way as any other discretionary trust – see Chapter 4. This means: gifts you make to these new trusts count as taxable gifts, so there could be a tax charge at the time the gift is made; and the assets in the trust come within the rules for periodic charges and exit charges.

❝ Bereaved minor's trust: provided the child takes over the trust assets completely by age 18, there is no IHT. ❞

Old accumulation-and-maintenance trusts

There is a breathing space before the new rules start to apply to accumulation-and-maintenance trusts already in existence on 22 March 2006. So the old, more favourable rules continue until 5 April 2008. If you do nothing, the new rules then kick in from 6 April 2008 onwards.

 Deciding whether or not to alter an existing accumulation-and-maintenance trust is a complex issue. Get advice from a solicitor, tax adviser or independent financial adviser.

Alternatively, the old rules can continue to apply for the life of the trust if you alter the trust so that all the beneficiaries take over the trust assets no later than age 18. In this case, the trust escapes the periodic and exit IHT charges.

A third option is to vary the terms of the trust, so that all the beneficiaries take over the trust assets by age 25. In this case, there will be no IHT on the trust up to the beneficiaries reaching age 18, but tax will apply for the period from age 18 to 25 – see box, right.

Planning point

If you set up an accumulation-and-maintenance trust before 22 March 2006, you have three choices:

- **Do nothing.** IHT will start to apply to the trust from 6 April 2008 onwards.
- **Alter the trust so that beneficiaries take over the assets by age 18.** IHT will not apply to the trust.
- **Alter the trust so that beneficiaries take over the assets by age 25.** IHT will apply only to the period from each beneficiary reaching age 18 to taking over the trust assets.

The 18–25 regime

If children do not take over trust assets completely by the time they reach 18, IHT may be charged on bereaved minor's trusts and old accumulation-and-maintenance trusts. The IHT charge applies at the time each child does take over the assets on or before their 25th birthday.

The charge is worked out in broadly the same way as a periodic charge (see page 86) but scaled down to reflect the period from the child reaching 18 to taking over the trust assets. For example, if the child receives the assets at age 25, the charge will be based on a period of seven years from age 18 to 25.

The *maximum* IHT rate will be 70% x periodic-charge rate = 4.2% of the value of the property leaving the trust. Often the actual rate will be lower.

" If you set up an accumulation-and-maintenance trust before 22 March 2006, you have three choices. "

95

Investments for children

The purpose of your gift and the amount will be big factors in determining the types of investments you choose for a child.

The investments you choose to give a child depend largely on the purpose of the investment, the amount involved and whether you want to invest on a regular basis or as a single lump sum, how long you want to invest, the amount of risk you are comfortable taking, and how the investment is taxed.

THE PURPOSE OF YOUR GIFT

The table below suggests some suitable investments depending on the purpose you have in mind.

Short-term aims

To encourage money-management skills or the savings habit, cash gifts direct to the child are likely to be best. These can be paid into a bank or building society account. Many providers offer accounts specifically for children with free gifts,

Investments for children

Aim of the gift	Suitable investments
Teach the child money-management skills	Bank or building society account Cash ISA (if child is age 16 or over)
Encourage the child to learn how to save	Bank or building society account NS&I investment account Cash ISA (if child is aged 16 or over)
Build up a nest-egg	Child trust fund NS&I children's bonus bonds NS&I premium bonds Friendly society tax-efficient plan Unit trusts and OEICs Investment trusts
Build up a pension	Stakeholder pension

96

regular magazines, and so on. It is important that the child has ready access to the account, so check out banks and building societies that have branches near the child's home.

Long-term aims

Building up a nest-egg for a child is normally a medium- to long-term aim (five to ten years or more). The most suitable choices for medium- to long-term goals are usually share-based investments. In the past, share-based investments have tended to produce higher returns than bank and building society accounts. But share-based investments involve capital risk. If you are not comfortable with this risk, stick to the safer investments such as cash-based child trust funds, savings accounts or NS&I children's bonus bonds.

A middling-risk option would be a stakeholder child trust fund. Another medium-risk option would be a friendly society tax-efficient plan (sometimes marketed as 'baby bonds') invested on a with-profits basis. However, government rules limit the maximum investment in these plans to £25 per month or £270 per year per person. With such a small amount, any flat-rate charges can eat heavily into the investment, so check the impact of charges carefully before you invest.

This leaves a share-based child trust fund or unit and investment trusts as the main choices for long-term growth. A child can't hold unit and investment trusts direct, however you can make the investment in your name but 'designated' for the child. This is normally enough to ensure that a bare trust is created, though to be sure you could write to your tax office stating your intention that the investment be treated as belonging to the child.

〈〈 The most suitable choices for medium- to long-term goals are usually share-based investments. 〉〉

Jargon buster

Capital risk The risk of losing some or all of the money you invest because the value of the investment can fall as well as rise

 If you are not sure which investments to choose, get advice from an independent financial adviser (IFA) – see page 212.

Planning point

Investing in a stakeholder pension scheme for a child is a very long-term gift but tax-efficient too. The amount you pay into the scheme qualifies for a bonus equal to basic rate tax relief on the contribution. So, at 2007-8 tax rates, for every £100 you give, HM Revenue & Customs adds a further £28.21.

Finally, if you are thinking very long term indeed, you can pay up to £2,808 a year into a stakeholder pension scheme for a child. This limit applies per recipient, so if you want to make gifts to several children you could pay in up to £2,808 a year for each of them. The child will not usually be able to take any proceeds from the scheme until he or she has reached at least age 55.

" If you are thinking very long term indeed, you can pay up to £2,808 a year into a stakeholder pension scheme. "

LOWER RISK INVESTMENTS IN DETAIL

With these investments, there is little or no risk of losing the amount originally invested, but over the long term the return tends to be lower than for higher-risk investments.

Bank and building society children's accounts

- **Description/suitable for** Accounts especially for children, usually offering introductory gifts, magazines, and so on. Useful as a way of teaching children how to manage money and getting them into the savings habit.
- **Return and charges** Interest, usually variable, on the amount invested. No explicit charges.
- **How long you invest for** Usually these are instant access accounts.
- **Minimum and maximum investment** Usually from £1. Usually no upper limit.
- **Tax** Interest usually paid with income tax at the savings rate already deducted. Children can usually reclaim this or arrange to be paid gross interest. But watch out if this is a gift from a parent (see page 90).

To compare the various stakeholder pensions on the market, use the Financial Services Authority comparative tables at www.fsa.gov.uk/tables or by calling 0845 606 1234.

Cash ISAs

- **Description/suitable for** Savings account that pays tax-free interest. Many are instant access accounts. Must be aged at least 16.
- **Return and charges** Interest on the amount invested. This is often variable, but occasionally fixed. Interest rates may be tiered with higher rates paid on larger balances. No explicit charges.
- **How long you invest for** For instant access accounts there is no set period. For other types of accounts, check the conditions.
- **Minimum and maximum investment** Often from £1. £3,000 a year upper limit set by the tax rules (£3,200 from 6 April 2008).
- **Tax** Tax-free interest.
- **How to invest** Contact provider, which may be a bank, building society or NS&I. You cannot hold an ISA on behalf of someone else (such as a child).

NS&I children's bonus bonds

- **Description/suitable for** Bonds that can be bought by anyone aged 16 and over for someone aged 16 or less. Useful as a way of giving a small nest-egg to a child.

- **Return and charges** Fixed return made up of interest and bonus added at end of term. Fixed return means the child would miss out if competing interest rates rose. No explicit charges.
- **How long you invest for** Five-year term. The child can have the money back early, but then loses interest. At the end of five years, you can reinvest for a new fixed return over five years, provided the child is still under age 16. Bonds must be cashed by age 21.
- **Minimum and maximum investment** From £25 up to £3,000 per issue per child.
- **Tax** Interest is tax-free.
- **How to invest** NS&I or through post offices.

What is meant by 'lower risk'

There is either very low or no capital risk with the investments in this section. National Savings & Investments (NS&I) products are ultimately backed by the government, so there is no risk. Banks and building societies must belong to the Financial Services Compensation Scheme, which covers the first £2,000 of any losses in full and 90 per cent of the next £33,000 in the unusual event of a bank or society going bust.

For information about National Savings & Investments products, visit its website at www.nsandi.com.

Giving to children

99

NS&I premium bonds

- **Description/suitable for** Bonds that give you the chance to win prizes by, in effect, gambling with the interest you would otherwise have earned.
- **Return and charges** Prizes ranging from £50 up to £1 million. Random prize draw is held every month. Each £1 invested counts as a separate bond and has a chance to win. If winnings are not reinvested, or winnings are small, your capital is vulnerable to inflation risk. No explicit charges.
- **How long you invest for** No set period.
- **Minimum and maximum investment** £100 up to £30,000 including reinvested prizes.
- **Tax** Prizes are tax-free.
- **How to invest** NS&I or through post offices. Bonds can be bought on behalf of children by parents and grandparents.

" For a child trust fund: parents and others can add up to £1,200 a year. "

Cash child trust fund (CTF)

- **Description/suitable for** Scheme for children born on or after 1 September 2002. The government provides vouchers (£250 at birth topped up to £500 for children in low-income families and similar amounts at age seven and possibly on entering

secondary school). These are invested in the child trust fund and must be left untouched until the child reaches 18. Parents, friends and anyone else can add to the fund. At 18, the young person can use the fund in any way they choose. The government has announced that, at 18, the fund can be rolled over into an ISA if the child wants to continue with tax-favoured saving. Parents choose how to invest the fund by opting for the cash version described here, a stakeholder CTF (see opposite) or a share-based CTF (see page 102). If parents fail to open a CTF within a year of receiving the vouchers, HM Revenue & Customs selects a stakeholder CTF for the child. The child can have only one CTF at a time but can switch from one CTF to another (either with the same or a different provider) at any time.

- **Return and charges** Interest is added. Usually variable. Lump sum paid out at age 18. No explicit charges. May be charges or loss of bonus on switching.
- **How long you invest for** Until age 18.
- **Minimum and maximum investment** Minimum is the government vouchers. Parents and others can add up to £1,200 a year extra.
- **Tax** Interest is tax-free.
- **How to invest** Contact the provider, which may be a bank or building society. For a full list of providers, see box, below.

The HM Revenue & Customs child trust fund website is at www.hmrc.gov.uk/ctf/. It includes a full list of providers.

100

HIGHER RISK INVESTMENTS IN DETAIL

The value of these investments can fall as well as rise, but they tend to give better returns over the long term than safer investments.

Stakeholder child trust fund (CTF)

- **Description/suitable for** Scheme generally as for cash CTFs (see opposite). To use the name 'stakeholder', this type of CTF must meet various conditions concerning, for example, the way it is invested and charges.
- **Return and charges** Pay-out and options at 18 as for cash CTF. Charges must come to no more than 1.5 per cent a year of the value of investments in the fund. There must be no charge for switching into or out of a stakeholder CTF.
- **Risk** Medium risk. Many stakeholder CTFs work basically like unit trusts (see page 103). A stakeholder CTF must be invested in a range of assets, including stock-market investments. The aim is to balance a reasonable chance of long-term growth with a controlled level of capital risk. The fund must also be 'lifestyled', which means that, from age 13 onwards, the fund shifts out of stock market investments and into safer deposits in order to lock in gains and protect against the effects of any sharp fall in the stock market as the child approaches age 18.
- **How long you invest for** Until age 18.
- **Minimum and maximum investment** As for cash CTFs (see opposite).

A stakeholder CTF must accept amounts as low as £10.
- **Tax** There is no tax for the investor to pay. Investments in the underlying fund build up largely tax-free but dividends from shares and similar income has had tax at 10 per cent deducted and this cannot be reclaimed.
- **How to invest** Through direct contact with providers, which are mainly banks, friendly societies and fund managers or through an IFA. However, all CTF providers must offer the option of a stakeholder CTF, so banks and building societies offering cash CTFs will also offer access to a stakeholder CTF sometimes from another provider. For a full list of providers, see the HM Revenue & Customs child trust fund website (see box, opposite).

❝A stakeholder CTF must be invested in a range of assets. The aim is to balance a reasonable chance of long-term growth with a controlled level of capital risk. ❞

Friendly society tax-efficient plans
- **Description/suitable for** Friendly societies are similar to insurance companies and generally offer similar types of product. But friendly societies are able to offer small savings plans that give a largely tax-free return (in contrast to most insurance policies where the insurance company has

101

Giving to children

already paid tax on the return from the underlying investments). Useful as a way of building up a small nest-egg. Some of these plans are specifically marketed as investments for children.

- **Return and charges** The plan usually pays out a lump sum after a set number of years, for example ten. Usually, there is an administration fee when you invest. If the plan is invested on a unit-linked basis (similar to a unit trust), there is also usually an initial charge (up to, say, 5 per cent) and an annual management charge (for example, 1.5 per cent a year of the value of the investment fund) with other costs charged direct to the fund. If the plan is invested on a with-profits basis (see box, overleaf), charges influence the level of bonuses.
- **Risk** Capital risk varies depending on the underlying investments.
- **How long you invest for** Usually you must invest for at least ten years. If you cash in your investment early, surrender charges reduce the amount you get back – perhaps to even less than you had invested.
- **Minimum and maximum investment** Minimum varies from one society to another. Maximum set by tax rules at £25 a month or £270 a year.
- **Tax** There is no tax for the investor to pay and the investments in the underlying fund build up largely

tax-free, but dividends from shares and similar income has had tax at 10 per cent deducted and this cannot be reclaimed.
- **How to invest** Through direct contact with friendly societies or via an IFA.

Share-based child trust fund

- **Description/suitable for** As for cash CTFs (see page 100).
- **Return and charges** Pay-out and options at 18 as for cash CTF. Usually an up-front charge (up to 5 per cent or so of the amount invested) and an annual management charge (generally from 0.5 up to 1.5 per cent a year of the value of the fund). Other charges are deducted direct from the fund. Often charges for switching between funds.
- **Risk** Medium to high risk. Many work basically like unit trusts (see opposite).
- **How long you invest for** Until age 18.
- **Minimum and maximum investment** As for cash CTFs (see page 100). But minimum varies from one provider to another, for example, £10 to £100 for regular sums and £10 to £500 as one-off amounts.
- **Tax** As for stakeholder CTFs (see page 101).
- **How to invest** Through direct contact with providers who are mainly friendly societies, fund managers and stockbrokers or through an IFA.

For a full list of providers, see the HM Revenue & Customs child trust fund website: www.hmrc.gov.uk/ctf/.

102

Share-based unit trusts and open-ended investment companies (OEICS)

- **Description/suitable for** You buy 'units' in a unit trust (or shares in an OEIC) which give you a stake in an investment fund. The fund is a ready-made portfolio of many different shares. You can choose funds that aim to produce income and/or growth.
- **Return and charges** The return takes the form of income distributions usually paid/credited every six months and/or, if you sell your units for more than you paid, a capital gain. You can choose growth funds that pay low or no distributions. There is usually an up-front charge (up to 5 per cent or so of the amount you invest) and an annual management charge (usually around 1 to 1.5 per cent a year of the value of your investment). Other charges are deducted direct from the investment fund.
- **Risk** The price of your units can fall as well as rise, so you are exposed to capital risk.
- **How long you invest for** No set period but because the value of the investment fund can fall as well as rise you should normally aim to invest for the long term (more than five years).
- **Minimum and maximum investment** Varies from, say, £500 or more as a lump sum and £50 per month for regular savings. No maximum.
- **Tax** Distributions are paid with tax at 10 per cent already deducted. Non-taxpayers, such as most children, cannot reclaim this tax. Capital gains

are taxable, the child is likely to have unused allowance in which case there will be no tax to pay. Watch out if gift from a parent (see page 90).
- **How to invest** You can go to the provider direct, but you'll often pay less in charges if you go to a discount broker or fund supermarket. You can also invest through most IFAs and many stockbrokers.

> **Stakeholder pension schemes: anyone - even a child - can have a scheme. Other people can invest in your scheme on your behalf.**

Stakeholder pension schemes

- **Description/suitable for** A way of saving for retirement. Anyone – even a child – can have a scheme. Other people can invest in your scheme on your behalf. Money invested early in life has a long time to grow so makes a particularly valuable contribution towards retirement savings.
- **Return and charges** Your money can be invested either on a unit-linked basis (similar to unit trusts) or a with-profits basis (see box, overleaf).
- **Risk** Capital risk varies depending on the underlying investments.
- **How long you invest for** Until at least age 55.
- **Minimum and maximum investment** From £20, whether this is a regular contribution or a lump sum up to

103

£2,808 a year (unless the child has earnings, in which case more can be invested).
- **Tax** The government adds basic-rate tax relief to the contributions (even for a non-taxpayer). Gains and most of the income from investing the contributions are tax-free. But income from shares and similar investments has had tax at 10 per cent deducted and this cannot be reclaimed. Part of the proceeds can be drawn as a tax-free lump sum; the rest must be taken as taxable pension.
- **How to invest** Through direct contact with pension providers or via an IFA.

With-profits investments

Your savings grow through the addition of yearly bonuses which, once added, can't usually be taken back. The size of bonuses depends largely on the growth of an underlying investment fund, which is typically invested in shares, bonds, property and cash. Bonuses are smoothed by keeping back in reserve some growth from good years to top up your return in poor years. An extra 'terminal' bonus is also added when the policy matures. You are not totally protected from large stock market swings because, if you cash in your policy early and investment returns have been poor, the provider can deduct a charge (called a 'market value reduction' or MVR).

❝Stakeholder pension schemes: the government adds basic-rate tax relief to the contributions (even for a non-taxpayer). ❞

Investment trusts

These give you a stake in an investment fund and so are an alternative to investing in unit trusts or OEICs, but work in a different way. You invest by buying the shares of the investment trust company.

104

Giving to charity

Gifts to charity in your lifetime and on death are free of capital gains tax and inheritance tax. More than that, you can arrange lifetime gifts to charity so they qualify for income tax relief. And a careful choice of gift can even save you capital gains tax.

Cash donations to charity

By arranging your donations to charity tax-efficiently, you benefit the charity as well as yourself.

GIFT AID

Gift aid is a scheme to encourage you to make donations to charity by giving you tax relief on the amount you give. You can get tax relief up to your highest rate on money you give to charity or a community amateur sports club through the gift aid scheme. You can make gifts of any amount this way.

The amount you give is treated as having had tax relief at the basic rate (22 per cent in 2007–8 falling to 20 per cent in 2008–9) already deducted. The charity then claims the tax relief from the HM Revenue & Customs and adds it to your gift. In this way, every £10 you give in 2007–8 is worth £10 / (100% – 22%) = £12.82 to the charity. Put another way: for every £10 you want the charity to receive, you pay only £7.80 – the government pays the rest.

If you are a higher-rate taxpayer, you can claim extra tax relief on a gift aid donation equal to the difference between relief at the higher rate (40 per cent in 2007–8) and the basic-rate relief you have already deducted from the gift. Higher-rate relief is either given through an adjustment to your pay-as-you-earn (PAYE) code or through the self-assessment system.

To use the gift aid scheme you simply need to make a declaration that includes:

- The name of the charity
- A description of the gift
- Your name
- Your address including your postcode.

The declaration should normally be in writing but does not have to be on any special form and can be made in any way, including fax or internet. The declaration can cover a single gift or series of gifts if you are making regular donations.

Alternatively, if you are making a donation by phone, you can give the details orally. The charity no longer has to send you a written record of your declaration unless you ask for one.

Tax advantages for charities

An organisation with charitable status is eligible for a variety of tax benefits. As long as it meets certain conditions, it currently enjoys complete freedom from income tax, capital gains tax (CGT) and corporation tax on its income and profits from most sources. In addition, when it receives donations, the charity may be able to claim back income tax that has been paid by the giver through the gift aid scheme.

Case Study Naveed

Following the death of a close friend from cancer, Naveed gives £78 to Cancer Research UK in 2007-8. He makes the donation by phone. The charity asks him for his name and address and to confirm that he is a taxpayer. Naveed asks for a copy of these details and receives them a few days later. The charity is able to claim back basic-rate tax relief of £78 x 22% / (100% - 22%) = £22, bringing the total it receives to £100. Through his self-assessment tax return, Naveed claims higher-rate relief which comes to 40% x £100 - £22 = £18. The charity has received £100 at a cost to Naveed of just £78 - £18 = £60.

Gift aid and age allowance

If you're aged 65 or over, you qualify for a higher age-related personal allowance (often called 'age allowance') – see the table, overleaf. And, if you are a married man and you or your wife were born before 6 April 1935, you can qualify for married couple's allowance, which includes an age-related addition. However, if your 'total income' exceeds a given limit (£20,900 in 2007–8), your age-related allowances are reduced until they reach a basic amount. The rate of reduction is £1 for every £2 by which total income exceeds the limit.

'Total income' is basically your income from most sources, excluding tax-free income (for example, from individual savings accounts (ISAs) or National Savings & Investments Certificates) less certain expenses that qualify for tax relief. Gift aid donations are one such expense.

If you are in the income bracket where you are losing (or have just lost) age allowance – see the table, overleaf – making donations by gift aid is especially tax-efficient. In addition to the charity claiming back relief on your gift, you will get an increase in your allowance that will reduce your tax bill.

Case Study Stan

Stan is 76 and a widower. In 2007-8, Stan has an income of £25,830 from his state and private pensions. This is too high for him to qualify for any age-related personal allowance, so he gets just the basic personal allowance of £5,225. His tax bill for the year is £4,265.50.

But then Stan decides to give £156 to the Royal Naval Benevolent Trust. The charity is able to claim back £156 x 22% / (100% - 22%) = £44, so the 'grossed-up' donation is £156 + £44 = £200. This reduces Stan's 'total income' to £25,830 - £200 = £25,630. This is £25,630 - £20,900 = £4,730 more than the age allowance income limit and means the maximum age allowance for someone of his age of £7,690 is reduced by £4,730 / 2 = £2,365, bringing the allowance to £5,325 - slightly more than the basic allowance.

As a result, Stan's tax bill falls to £4,243.50. Stan saves £22 in tax. In other words, the charity gets £200 at a total cost to Stan of £134.

107

Age allowance and the income limit at which it is lost in 2007-8

Age you reach during the tax year	If you are married, age your wife reaches during the tax year	Maximum personal allowance	Maximum married couple's allowance	Income limit at which extra age-related allowances lost [1]
If you are a single person or a married woman [2]				
Under 65	Not applicable	£5,225	Not applicable	Not applicable
65 to 74	Not applicable	£7,550	Not applicable	£25,550
75 or over	Not applicable	£7,690	Not applicable	£25,830
If you are a married man [2]				
Under 65	Under 73	£5,225	Not applicable	Not applicable
	73 or 74	£5,225	£6,285	£28,590
	75 or over	£5,225	£6,365	£28,750
65 to 72	Under 73	£7,550	Not applicable	£25,550
	73 or 74	£7,550	£6,285	£33,240
	75 or over	£7,550	£6,365	£33,400
73 or 74	Under 75	£7,550	£6,285	£33,240
	75 or over	£7,550	£6,365	£33,400
75 or over	Any age	£7,690	£6,365	£33,680

[1] You start to lose age allowance at a rate of £1 for every £2 of income over £20,900 in 2007-8.
[2] If you were married before 5 December 2005, the age-related part of the married couple's allowance is always awarded to the husband and reduced in accordance with his income. For couples married on or after 5 December 2005 and for civil partners, the age-related part is awarded to the spouse or partner with the highest income – if this applies to you, in this table for 'married woman' read 'the person with the lower income' and for 'married man' read 'the person with the higher income'.

Covenants

A covenant is a legally binding promise to give something to someone (or to do or refrain from doing something). In the past, it has been a common way of agreeing to make regular donations to a charity and, providing certain conditions were met, the donations qualified for tax relief under rules that applied specifically to covenants. Since April 2000 onwards, the special rules no longer apply. Instead, covenanted donations come under the normal rules for gift aid. You can still make gifts by deed of covenant if you want to, but there is no tax reason for doing so.

Gift aid and tax credits

Working tax credit and child tax credit are state benefits that are integrated with the tax system in the sense that the amount of credit you can get depends broadly on your income for tax purposes. If you are a couple, credits are based on your joint income.

Gift aid donations are deducted from your income in assessing how much you qualify for in tax credits.

Working tax credit is designed to help people who work but have only a low income. Households with no children would be unlikely to qualify if their income exceeds around £11,800 (single person) or £16,400 (couple) in 2007–8.

Households with children can qualify for child tax credit and, if they are in work, working tax credit too. They can continue to be entitled to credits up to much higher levels of income than childless people. In 2007–8 you can get at least some child tax credit if your income is up to £58,175 (or £66,350 if you have a child under one year old).

In particular, a basic family element of child tax credit equal to £545 in 2007–8 (or £1,090 if you have a child under one year old) is paid until your household income reaches £50,000. The family element is then reduced by £1 for every £15 above that limit. Therefore, if your income is above £50,000, a gift aid donation can be very tax-efficient if it also increases the child tax credit you get (see the case study, below).

Planning point

Gift aid donations can be especially tax efficient if you are getting age allowance or tax credits. As well as tax relief on the donation, your tax allowance or tax credits may also increase.

❝ If your income is above £50,000, a gift aid donation can be very tax-efficient. ❞

Case Study   Andrea and Bob

Andrea and Bob have one child and an income of £53,000 in 2007-8. The full tax credit is £545 but this is reduced by (£53,000 - £50,000) / £15 = £200 to £345.

If Bob gives £500 to charity through gift aid, the charity receives £500 / (100% - 22%) = £641.03. Bob is a higher-rate taxpayer and so also gets higher-rate tax relief of (40% - 22%) x £641.03 = £115.38.

The couple's income for child tax

credit is also reduced by the gross gift aid donation (rounded up to the nearest £1) to £53,000 - £642 = £52,358. Their child tax credit is now reduced by only (£52,358 - £50,000) / £15 = £157.20 to £387.80.

In total, tax relief and extra credit come to £299.21 which is 46.7 per cent of the gross gift aid donation. Looked at another way, the charity gets £641.03 at a cost to Bob and Andrea of just £341.82.

109

Carrying back gift aid donations

For gift aid donations made on or after 6 April 2003, you can elect to have the gift treated for tax purposes as if it had been paid in the previous tax year.

Your election must be made to HM Revenue & Customs in writing on or before the date on which you deliver your tax return for the year to which the donation is being carried back. There is space on the tax return to make this election.

For example, suppose you make a donation during 2007–8 that you want to carry back to the 2006–7 tax year. Your tax return for 2006–7 must be filed no later than 31 January 2008. This means you have until 31 January 2008 to both pay the donation and file your return. You cannot carry back the donation if you make it after 31 January 2008. If you file your return early – say, by 30 September 2007 – you cannot carry back a donation made after that date.

To use the carry back election, you must have either income or capital gains in the earlier year on which you have paid tax.

Using the election affects only the tax relief you get and not the amount that can be reclaimed by the charity or sports club. It still claims back relief based on the basic tax rate for the year in which the donation was actually paid.

Carrying back a donation means you can claim any higher rate tax relief more quickly and might save you tax in the following situations:

- You are a non-taxpayer or starting-rate taxpayer this tax year but paid tax at the basic or higher rate last year.
- You are a basic-rate taxpayer this year but paid tax at the higher rate last year.
- Your income last tax year was in the range where you were losing age allowance.

Carrying back a gift aid donation does not affect a claim for tax credits because for this purpose the donation continues to be deductible for the year the donation was paid, not the year to which it was carried back.

Case Study **Jess**

In June 2007, Jess gives £250 to the Red Cross. After claiming tax relief, the Red Cross receives £320.51. Jess is a basic-rate taxpayer in 2007-8, so in the normal way there would be no further tax relief to come. But Jess was a higher-rate taxpayer in the previous tax year (2006-7). In January 2008, she is completing her 2006-7 tax return and elects to use the carry back rule so that her June 2007 donation is treated as if it had been paid in 2006-7. This means Jess qualifies for higher-rate tax relief of £57.91, which is given as a reduction in her tax bill for 2006-7.

110

Donating a tax rebate to charity

You can also use your tax return to elect that all or up to a set amount of any tax rebate is donated to a single charity of your choice. The Revenue will then automatically pass the rebate to the charity you have selected.

You can opt for the donation to be made using gift aid by ticking the appropriate box on the tax return. The charity will then be able to claim back basic-rate tax relief when it receives the donation.

If you are a higher-rate taxpayer, you claim higher-rate tax relief on the donation through the next year's tax return. For example, if you are completing your tax return for 2006–7 and opt to donate a rebate of tax paid in 2006–7, you claim higher-rate relief through your 2007–8 tax return (which you will normally receive in April 2008 and must send back by 31 January 2009).

Gift aid if you pay little or no tax

Do not use gift aid if you are a non-taxpayer or will have only a very low income tax and/or CGT bill for the year in which you pay the donation (or the year to which you elect to carry it back).

If you are a non-taxpayer, the charity will still claim the relief from HM Revenue & Customs. But HMRC will then ask you for tax equal to the relief given. Similarly, if your tax bill for the year is less than the amount of tax relief that you are treated as having deducted from your donation, the charity will still claim

full tax relief on the donation, but HMRC will ask you for tax equal to the excess relief given.

❝ Do not use gift aid if you are a non-taxpayer: the charity will still claim the relief from HM Revenue & Customs. But HMRC will then ask you for tax equal to the relief given. ❞

111

Other points to note about gift aid

Your gift will not qualify for gift aid if you (or someone connected with you, such as a family member) in return get some benefit as a result of the gift and the benefit exceeds the limits shown in the table, below. But you can ignore the following benefits:

- The right to free or reduced-price entry to properties preserved for the public benefit, where maintaining such properties is the main or sole purpose of the charity and the opportunity to benefit is publicly available.
- The right to free or reduced-price entry to observe wildlife, where the conservation of such wildlife is the sole or main purpose of the charity and the opportunity to benefit is publicly available.

Case Study June

June is not a regular churchgoer but likes to go to a service from time to time. Last Sunday, she noticed a pile of envelopes as she entered the church with 'Gift Aid' printed across the top. The steward explained that, provided she was a taxpayer, instead of just putting cash direct on the collection plate, she could first put her offering in one of these envelopes, filling in the form on the front. That way the church could claim back tax relief on whatever she gave. June put £3 in the envelope. The church can claim back £3 x 22% / (100% - 22%) = 85p, bringing the total offering to £3.85 at a cost to Mary of just £3. Multiplied across its whole congregation, gift aid is a valuable source of extra funds for the church.

Maximum benefit for gift aid

Size of your gift	Maximum benefit allowed	Example
up to £100	25% of the value of the gift	You give £50, any benefit must be worth no more than £50 x 25% = £12.50
Over £100 up to £1,000	£25	You give £500. The maximum benefit is £25
Over £1,000	5% (2.5% before 6 April 2007) of the value of the gift	You give £1,500. Any benefit must be worth no more than £1,500 x 5% = £75
AND All gifts to the same charity during the same tax year	£500 (£250 before 6 April 2007)	You make 40 gifts of £100 to the same charity. In line with the rule above, 25% of each gift would give a total potential benefit of 40 x £25 = £1,000 but this rule caps the benefit at £500

112

PAYROLL GIVING SCHEMES

Payroll giving (also called 'Payroll deduction') is a method of making regular gifts to charity out of your salary. It is open only to employees and only to those whose employer operates a payroll giving scheme. You can give any amount using this scheme.

The scheme works like this. Your employer sets up an arrangement with an agency approved by the HM Revenue & Customs (in fact, a few employers have set up their own agencies).

You then tell your employer how much you want to give each payday and to which charity or charities. The employer deducts the specified amount from your pay and hands it over to the agency, which arranges for the money to be transferred to the charities you picked. The agency may make a charge – for example, 5 per cent of the donations it handles – to cover its own running costs, but sometimes there is no charge or your employer might separately cover any administration costs.

Your donation is deducted from your pay before tax (but not National Insurance) is worked out, so you automatically get full income tax relief. Payroll giving is popular with charities because they receive the whole (gross) donation direct from you, avoiding any paperwork and delay involved in claiming tax relief from HMRC as they have to with gift aid.

Case Study — Mary

Mary earns £810 a month, before tax, working in the local supermarket. The supermarket operates a payroll giving scheme through which Mary gives £10 a month each to Help the Aged and Barnardo's. Normally, Mary would pay £60.11 a month in income tax (during the 2007-8 tax year), but after deducting the payroll giving from her pay, the tax bill is reduced to £55.71 a month. In other words, she gets tax relief of £4.40 a month, which reduces the cost to her of the £20 she gives to charity to just £15.60.

If your employer operates a payroll giving scheme, he or she can provide you with details and an application form. You do not have to keep up your donations for any minimum period of time. You stop making them whenever you like simply by informing your employer of your wishes.

Payroll giving cannot be used in combination with any of the other tax-advantageous ways of giving to charity. So, for example, you cannot claim gift aid relief on donations made through a payroll giving scheme. HM Revenue & Customs rules do not allow payroll giving to be used to pay subscriptions entitling you, for example, to membership benefits from a charity.

 One of the largest agencies running payroll giving schemes is the Charities Aid Foundation (CAF) - www.cafonline.org - which operates a scheme called Give As You Earn (GAYE).

Giving to charity

113

Other donations

You do not have to donate cash to charities. You could instead give something you own: for example, land, premises, a car, furniture or investments such as shares.

Normally you might have to pay CGT and even IHT when you give something away. But gifts to charities and, from 6 April 2002, community amateur sports clubs, are generally completely free of these taxes.

For the exemption from IHT to apply, you must relinquish all your rights to whatever it is that you are giving. For example, there might well be a tax bill if you gave the freehold of your home to a charity but continued to live there. For more details about the way CGT and IHT work, see Chapter 3.

In addition to the CGT and IHT reliefs described above, gifts of some types of assets to charities – but not community amateur sports clubs – can also qualify for income tax relief. Since 6 April 2000, this applies to gifts of shares and similar investments and, from 6 April 2002 onwards, it has also applied to gifts of land or buildings.

GIFTS OF SHARES OR SIMILAR INVESTMENTS

You can claim income tax relief when you give any of these investments to a charity:

- Shares or securities listed on a recognised stock exchange.
- Unlisted shares or securities dealt on a recognised stock exchange (including the Alternative Investment Market).
- Units in an authorised unit trust.
- Shares in an open-ended investment company (OEIC).
- An interest in an offshore investment fund.

You can claim the market value of the shares or units you give (plus any costs of disposal you incur) as a deduction from your income. This means you get income tax relief up to your top rate. If you receive anything for the shares

Planning point

Giving shares, unit trusts, land or property direct to charity, rather than selling them first and giving cash, can be very tax-efficient where you would stand to make a gain on the assets if they were sold. If the assets are standing at a loss, it can be more efficient to sell them first and give cash using the gift aid scheme.

114

or units – either cash or a benefit in kind – this is deducted from the amount you can claim.

This relief is available not only for gifts to charities but also to the National Heritage Memorial Fund, the Historic Buildings and Monuments Commission for England, the British Museum and the Natural History Museum.

Note that you can only claim this income tax relief against your income and not against any capital gains you make on other sales or gifts. This means that giving shares or units will not be tax-efficient if you do not have enough income against which to set the relief.

GIFTS OF LAND OR BUILDINGS

Income tax relief is available on a gift of land or buildings to charity – but not community amateur sports clubs – made on or after 6 April 2002. Giving land or buildings works in much the same way as giving shares (see above), so you can claim the market value of the property plus any disposal costs less anything you receive in exchange.

The property must be in the UK but can be either freehold or leasehold. You must completely give up your ownership rights and, if you own the property jointly with other people, you must surrender your rights to the charity.

In general, relief is withdrawn if, within five years of 31 January following the tax year in which you give the property away, you acquire any interest or right in the property. There are two

Giving to charity

Case Study Harry

Harry, who is a higher-rate taxpayer, wants to make a substantial donation to the Arthritis Research Campaign (ARC). He is considering funding his donation by selling some HBOS plc shares.

Harry could sell the shares for £2,500, of which £1,000 would be taxable. He has already used up his CGT allowance for the year (see page 42), so he would have to pay tax of 40% x £1,000 = £400. This would leave £2,500 – £400 = £2,100 to give to ARC. The gift would qualify for gift aid (see page 106), so ARC would claim back basic-rate tax relief on the £2,100 and Harry would get higher-rate relief on the gift. This would mean ARC received £2,692 in total at an overall cost to Harry of £2,100 + £400 – £485 = £2,015.

Instead, Harry could give the shares direct to ARC. There is no CGT to pay on gifts to charity. And Harry can claim income tax relief on the market value of the gift which is £2,500. This means Harry gets income tax relief of 40% x £2,500 = £1,000. The charity sells the shares to realise the full £2,500. In this way the charity gets £2,500 at a cost to Harry of £2,500 – £1,000 = £1,500. Therefore, giving the shares direct is the better option.

exceptions: first, if you acquire the interest through the death of someone; and second, if you pay the full going rate for the interest or right – for example, if you live in the property but pay the full market rent.

To claim the relief, you must have a certificate from the charity concerned describing the property, the date it was given and stating that the charity has accepted the gift.

115

Other ways of giving

In addition to tax incentives already described, there are several other arrangements you can use to ensure that both you and the charity get the most from your gifts.

CHARITABLE BEQUESTS

If you leave money or assets to charity in your will, your estate pays no IHT on the gift. (Your estate is all your possessions less any debts at the time of death.)

A bequest to charity can also save inheritance tax in a second way, because the value of your estate is reduced by the amount of your gift to charity. This can mean less IHT on the estate as a whole. Bear in mind, though, that making a bequest to charity cuts down the amount of the estate left for your heirs to inherit, so you should not use this as a tax-saving method unless you intend to make philanthropic gifts anyway.

All gifts from your estate when you die – whether to charity or to other organisations or to people – are free of CGT.

Some charities offer you help in making your will – for example, paying the cost – in the hope that you will leave something to the charity. For the will to

be legally watertight, it is essential that there can be no question of the charity having brought undue influence to bear on you. If it was thought that a charity had pressurised you into leaving it a bequest, your will could be challenged by other beneficiaries and, in the end, your gift to the charity might not be made after all. To avoid any problems of this sort, you should ensure that:

- You have written details of the arrangement by which the charity is helping you to make your will and the procedures to be followed.
- You do not proceed if the charity's help is conditional on your making it a bequest.
- The solicitor you use takes instructions from you alone and not the charity.
- No details of your will are disclosed to the charity without your consent.
- You do not proceed if you feel in any way pressurised to include the charity in your will.

 A solicitor can help you to insert an appropriate clause in your will to leave a bequest to charity. See also the *Which? Essential Guide* to *Wills and Probate*.

116

CAF CHARITY ACCOUNT

The Charities Aid Foundation (CAF) is a charity whose aim is to promote charities generally and give them support and assistance. One of the services it runs is the CAF Charity Account. This is like a bank account with the sole purpose of making gifts to charity. The advantages of the Charity Account are that the money you give is increased by tax relief and you have a convenient, flexible way of giving to a wide range of charities. CAF makes a charge for running the account. It works as follows.

You pay money into your Charity Account using the tax-efficient means already discussed: gift aid (see page 106), payroll giving (see page 113) or gifts of shares and similar investments (see page 114). Because CAF is itself a charity, it is able to claim tax relief on the money you pay in using gift aid and it adds this to your account. With payroll giving, you qualify for tax relief directly as normal. With gifts of shares, your gift is free of CGT and you can claim income tax relief. CAF sells the shares and then credits the proceeds to your account.

CAF sets minimum limits on the amount you can pay into the account of either £100 as a lump sum or £10 a month if you pay in regularly. In 2006, CAF's charges for running the account were 4 per cent of sums up to £15,000 and 1 per cent of any excess up to

£82,000, and a part of the amount you pay in is donated to the National Council for Voluntary Organisations (NCVO). If you pay into the account using payroll giving, your employer might agree to pay the charges. The money in the account does not earn interest.

You can make donations to any charity, whether registered or not. When you want to make a donation to charity from your account, you can do this in several ways:

- Online transfer, where you access your account over the internet and carry out a variety of transactions including making donations.
- Phone transfer.
- By post using a Charity Account chequebook.
- By standing order, if you want to make regular donations to a particular charity.

Note that you do not get any further tax relief when you make the donation, because it has already had the benefit of tax relief when you first paid the money into the Charity Account.

The normal rules that apply to gift aid and payroll giving apply when you are paying into the CAF Charity Account. For example, the CAF Charity Account is not suitable if you pay little or no tax and would receive a bill from HM Revenue & Customs for the tax relief paid over to CAF by gift aid (see page 111).

 For details of the Charities Aid Foundation (CAF) Charity Account or to find out about setting up a trust through CAF, see www.caf.org.uk.

117

Planning point

You can give flexibly and tax efficiently to charity by setting up your own charitable trust (which attracts favourable tax treatment). Normally, this is a costly and time-consuming business. But if you have at least £10,000 to invest, you can set up your own trust through the Charities Aid Foundation (CAF).

GIFTS FROM TRUSTS

A trust is a special legal arrangement where money, shares or other property are held for the benefit of others (see Chapter 4). Trustees have the duty of seeing that the property in the trust and any income and gains from it (which together make up the 'trust fund') are used as set out in the trust deed and rules. With a 'discretionary trust', the trustees are given the power to decide how the trust fund is used (within any constraints imposed by the trust rules).

Special tax rules apply to trusts (as described in Chapter 4), but gifts to charity from a discretionary trust can be very tax-efficient. The charity will be able to reclaim all the income tax – usually at 40 per cent (in 2007-8) rather than just the basic rate – that the trust has paid on the income it gives. If the trust makes a gift to charity of capital, there will be no CGT or IHT to pay.

DONATION CARDS (AFFINITY CARDS)

A number of charities and credit card companies have joined forces to issue donation cards (also called 'affinity cards'). These are normal credit cards but the card issuer promises to make donations to charity (or sometimes non-charitable groups, like football clubs) when you first take out the card and each time you use it. The donations are fairly small, for example, £10 when you take out the card and 5p each time you buy something using the card.

If you use a credit card anyway, a donation card is a way in which indirectly you can give to charity, but check that the card terms and conditions are competitive. If not, you would probably do better taking out a card that offers a better deal and using the money you save in interest or earn in cashback to make your own donations direct to charity using one of the tax-efficient schemes outlined in this chapter.

> **!** If you do not normally use a credit card, be wary of taking out a donation card. Do not risk putting yourself in a situation where you run up debts that you cannot afford.

118

Inheritance planning

Planning ahead for what happens after your death can help to ensure that your survivors are financially secure, your wealth is passed on to the people you choose and any tax bill is kept to a minimum. You might also want to consider steps to guard against the costs of long-term care ruining your inheritance plans.

Why plan for inheritance?

This chapter draws together a number of points already discussed and the strategies we will be looking at in the remaining chapters to show how you can plan your giving through inheritance more precisely and tax-efficiently.

There are two main aims to planning inheritance:

- To make sure that your estate is divided as you had wished.
- To minimise the amount of tax to be paid on the estate.

Clearly, the two aims are interlinked since lower IHT means more of your estate can be left to your family and friends. Strategies to meet either or both aims are summarised in this chapter and looked at in more detail in the chapters that follow.

Many more complex tax saving schemes aim to minimise tax on your estate at death by taking valuable assets out of your estate while still enabling you to use the assets during your lifetime without triggering the gift-with-reservation rules (see Chapter 4). The scope for this type of planning has been severely reduced by the introduction of the pre-owned assets tax (see Chapter 4) and the government's threat to introduce further 'retroactive' measures to counter successful tax avoidance schemes (see Chapter 1). Broadly, you would appear to be safe using tax-saving opportunities that are specifically allowed in the tax legislation (for example, making tax-free gifts, using your tax-free limit). But if you contemplate anything more complex, you should get professional advice and be aware that any tax savings could disappear if the scheme becomes the target of a change in tax law.

Always seek advice from, for example, a solicitor or accountant if you are in any doubt about a proposed course of action. And, if you are giving away large sums, get advice first.

120

The particular inheritance planning strategies you adopt will depend largely on your personal intentions and circumstances. Many can be applied simply and with a minimum of paperwork. Others are not so straightforward and may hide potential pitfalls that you should take into account, so it is crucial to get advice if your plans are at all complicated.

❝It is crucial to get advice if your plans are at all complicated.❞

Case Study Godfrey

Godfrey dies on 1 January 2008 leaving an estate of £280,000. He made the following gifts during his lifetime (assume the annual tax-free exemption has already been used each year):

1 January 1998	Taxable gift	£100,000 to a discretionary trust
1 January 2000	Taxable gift	£70,000 to a discretionary trust
1 February 2001	Taxable gift	£68,000 to a discretionary trust
1 June 2003	PET	£80,000 to his nephew, John

The PET was initially treated as a tax-free gift when it was made, but on Godfrey's death it is reassessed as a taxable gift. Therefore, the estate counts as a final gift of £280,000 in a running total of £68,000 + £80,000 + £280,000 = £428,000. The earlier gifts use up £148,000 of the £300,000 tax-free slice. £152,000 of the estate uses up the remaining part of the tax-free limit, leaving £128,000 of the estate to be taxed at 40 per cent – i.e. 40% x £128,000 = £51,200.

What happens to your estate if you don't plan?

If you die without a will, the law dictates who inherits your estate. The law favours husbands, wives, civil partners and children. However, other people – such as an unmarried partner – do not have any automatic rights to inherit. For more information on this subject, see Chapter 8 on pages 135–56.

121

What happens to inheritance tax if you don't plan?

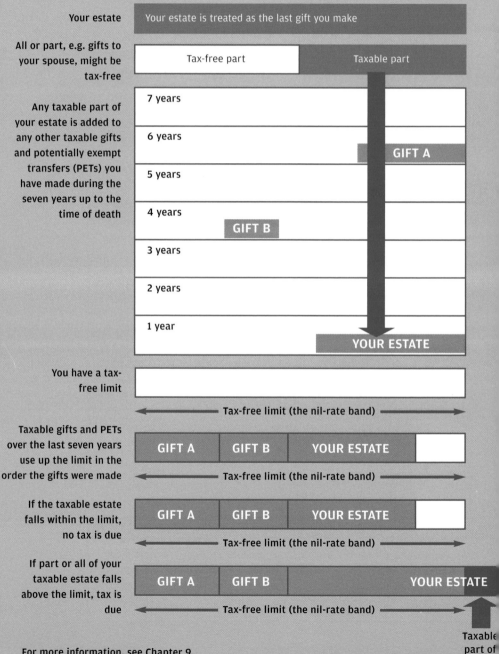

Your estate — Your estate is treated as the last gift you make

All or part, e.g. gifts to your spouse, might be tax-free

Tax-free part | Taxable part

Any taxable part of your estate is added to any other taxable gifts and potentially exempt transfers (PETs) you have made during the seven years up to the time of death

7 years
6 years — GIFT A
5 years
4 years — GIFT B
3 years
2 years
1 year — YOUR ESTATE

You have a tax-free limit

← Tax-free limit (the nil-rate band) →

Taxable gifts and PETs over the last seven years use up the limit in the order the gifts were made

GIFT A | GIFT B | YOUR ESTATE
← Tax-free limit (the nil-rate band) →

If the taxable estate falls within the limit, no tax is due

GIFT A | GIFT B | YOUR ESTATE
← Tax-free limit (the nil-rate band) →

If part or all of your taxable estate falls above the limit, tax is due

GIFT A | GIFT B | YOUR ESTATE
← Tax-free limit (the nil-rate band) →

Taxable part of estate

For more information, see Chapter 9.

Planning strategies

Here is a summary of the most commonly used strategies for inheritance planning.

GIFTS WHEN YOU DIE

By using your will, you can arrange to make tax-free gifts on death and to use your tax-free allowance.

Make tax-free gifts in your will

Some gifts you make on death are always free of IHT, for example, bequests to charity and whatever you leave to your husband, wife or civil partner (provided they are UK-domiciled – otherwise there is a limit of £55,000).

In addition to these and other gifts that are always tax-free, whether made on death or during your lifetime (see Chapter 2), there are a few gifts that are specifically tax-free on death only:

- Lump sum from a pension scheme, provided the trustees had discretion to decide who would receive it (though in practice they generally follow any nomination made by you). The lump sum by-passes your estate altogether and goes straight from the scheme to the recipient.
- Similarly the proceeds of a life insurance policy that was written in trust for the recipient. The proceeds by-pass the estate, going straight from the life insurance company to the recipient.

- The whole estate if the person died from a wound, accident or disease acquired or exacerbated while on active service against an enemy. To claim this exemption, the personal representatives need a certificate from the Ministry of Defence.
- Up to £10,000 received by the deceased as an ex-gratia payment to the survivors (or spouses of survivors) who were prisoners of war held by the Japanese during the Second World War.
- Amounts received by the victim (or his or her spouse) from specified schemes that provide compensation to people (such as Holocaust victims) for wrongs suffered during the Second World War.

Use your tax-free limit

Try to make use of your tax-free limit (which covers the first £300,000 of chargeable transfers in the 2007–8 tax year).

Bear in mind that some gifts – for example, to your husband, wife or civil partner or to charity – are always tax-free. It may be tempting simply to leave everything tax-free to your spouse or civil partner but this can mean an unnecessarily large tax bill later on when they die. Planning instead to use your tax-free limit can save as much as

123

40% x £300,000 = £120,000 in tax in 2007–8.

If you and your husband or wife intend to leave something to your children, it may be sensible to draw up your wills so that whoever dies first leaves part of the estate directly to the children. This will ensure that at least some use is made of the available tax-free limit. The remainder of the estate can be left to the surviving spouse. If you can, arrange the wills so that both of you can make maximum use of your tax-free limits but take care to ensure that the surviving spouse will have enough to meet financial needs.

Case Study Sam

In August 2007, Sam dies and leaves his whole estate of £250,000 to his wife, Harriet. Since this is a tax-free gift, there is no IHT to pay. When Harriet dies a few months later, her estate is valued at £350,000 and is left completely to their only child, Phyllis. There is IHT to pay on the estate calculated as follows:

Value of free estate	£350,000
less tax-free limit	£300,000
	£ 50,000
Tax on £50,000 @ 40%	£ 20,000

Instead Sam could have left £50,000 to Phyllis (on which no IHT would be payable because it would be covered by his tax-free limit) and the remaining £200,000 to Harriet. On Harriet's death, her estate would have been valued at £300,000. Giving this to Phyllis would have been completely covered by Harriet's tax-free limit, so no IHT would be payable. Straightforward planning to make use of Sam's tax-free limit would save £20,000 in tax.

Be aware of how gifts are taxed

If IHT is due on your estate, the tax does not usually fall evenly across all your heirs. Chapter 9 describes in detail how gifts you leave in your will are taxed in different ways. Briefly, there are three types of gift:

- **Tax-free gifts**, such as bequests to your husband or wife. None of the IHT on the estate may be paid from these gifts.
- **Gifts that bear their own tax**. A proportionate amount of the tax on the estate is deducted from each of these gifts before the remainder is paid to the recipient.
- **Free-of-tax gifts**. Although these are taxable gifts, tax on them is paid out of the residue of the estate, not the free-of-tax gifts themselves.

There are two important points that you should bear in mind when planning gifts under your will. First, a gift that bears its own tax will normally be smaller than a gift of the same size which is free-of-tax. Second, if you leave a lot of free-of-tax gifts, the residue of your estate may be reduced to a trivial amount (or nothing at all).

Jargon buster

Residue Whatever remains of your estate after all your debts, expenses and specific legacies and gifts have been made

124

Consider will trusts: an interest-in-possession trust

A trust set up under your will is deemed to start on the date of death. There are several situations in which setting up a trust in your will can be particularly useful.

The first is where you want to give some of your assets to the next generation but your wife, husband or civil partner will carry on needing the income from, or use of, those assets. One way around this is to leave the assets in trust, giving, say, your spouse an interest in possession during his or her lifetime, with your children (or perhaps their children) holding the reversionary interest (see page 80).

But note that, while this ensures that your assets are used largely as you would wish, it does not have any inheritance tax advantage over making an outright gift if, under the new tax rules for trusts (see Chapter 5), the trust counts as an 'immediate post-death interest (IPDI) trust'. This means that, although it generally qualifies for favourable inheritance tax treatment (see page 87), the person with an interest in possession is treated as if they own the underlying trust assets. They are then treated as if they give the assets away when the interest ends. So, if the trust ends on that person's death, the trust assets count as part of that person's estate, so there could be a large inheritance bill at the time of this second death.

There are two ways you could avoid this problem. First, you could instead set up a discretionary trust (see below). Second, you could set up an interest-in-

possession trust in your will that does not meet all the conditions necessary for it to qualify as an IPDI trust (get advice from your solicitor on how to do this). In both cases, the gift in your will is taxable and so can use up all or part of your tax-free limit, and the trust assets will not count as part of your spouse's or civil partner's estate so will not contribute towards a tax bill on their death.

Consider will trusts: a discretionary trust

Under IHT law, you can use your will to set up a discretionary trust. This can be tax-efficient provided the transfer of assets into the trust is covered by your tax-free limit at the time of death (or one of the other exemptions).

For example, you could leave an amount up to your tax-free limit to a discretionary trust with both your spouse and your children named as beneficiaries.

Inheritance planning

125

The trustees would have discretion over how the trust property and any income from it were used. You could informally, prior to death, make known to the trustees your hope that the assets could be largely preserved to be handed down to your children, but the trustees would not be bound to follow your wishes.

A discretionary will trust does not work so well where the main asset in your estate is your family home. Leaving part of your home to the trust and part to your partner means that your partner does not have free use of the family home. A solution might be to set up an IOU discretionary will trust. Under this arrangement, your partner buys the trust's share of the house but, assuming he or she does not have ready cash to pay the purchase price, instead gives the trust an IOU. This means the trust is lending money to your spouse or civil partner. The whole home passes to your partner who can use it freely during their lifetime (and move home if they choose). On your partner's death, the trust calls in the loan, which usually would be repaid by selling the home. For this plan to work efficiently, it is very important that the wording of the trust is precise and essential that you get professional advice. Under the new rules for trusts, a simpler option now may be to set up an interest-in-possession trust in your will, provided it does not count as an IPDI trust (see above).

Another way to use a discretionary will trust is as a device for devolving decisions to others who can make them in the light of the actual circumstances at the time of your death. Provided the property in a discretionary will trust is distributed within two years of your death, the gifts from the trust can be treated for inheritance tax purposes as if they had been bequests under your will. This can be particularly useful if, say, you hope to make bequests direct to your children in order to use your tax-free limit as described on page 124 but you are not sure at present whether your husband or wife would be able to manage on your remaining estate. Your will could direct that an amount up to the tax-free limit be left in trust with, say, your children and surviving spouse as potential beneficiaries. The trustees could then distribute the trust property taking into account the needs of your spouse at that time.

Case Study Sam

In August 2007, Sam dies, leaving an estate worth £350,000. He has left an amount equal to the tax-free limit (£300,000 at the time he dies) to a discretionary will trust and the residue of £50,000 to his wife.

The £300,000 left to the trust is a taxable gift but there is no tax to pay because it is covered by Sam's tax-free limit. The £50,000 to his wife is tax-free.

The beneficiaries of the trust are Sam's wife, Harriet, and his daughter, Phyllis. The trustees weigh up the needs of the beneficiaries and decide to pay £50,000 to Phyllis and give the remainder of the trust assets to Harriet. The trust is wound up and, as this is all completed within two years of Sam dying, the bequests are treated as if they had been made direct by Sam.

126

Planning point

Another important planning use of will trusts is where you are passing on your business. Rather than pass total control to, for example, a relatively inexperienced son or daughter, or to a spouse who is not involved in the business, it may make sense to put the land or property used by the business into trust. Provided the assets transferred to the trust qualify for business property relief or agricultural property relief, they pass to the trust free of IHT and the trust will also qualify for the same reliefs. This is a complex area and you should seek the advice of your accountant and/or solicitor.

USING LIFETIME GIFTS

One way to reduce the IHT payable on your death is to reduce the size of your estate by making gifts during your lifetime. However, before going down this road, you must consider your own financial needs.

Any IHT payable on your estate is a problem for your heirs, not you. IHT on your estate reduces the amount by which others benefit from what you leave, but does not affect you in your lifetime. It is not worth jeopardising your financial security in order to reduce the IHT bill of your heirs.

Assuming that you can afford to make a number of gifts during your lifetime, you will obviously want to ensure that they do not themselves give rise to a large tax bill. Chapter 2 lists the gifts that you can make during your lifetime that are tax-free.

It is not enough to look only at the IHT position of lifetime gifts. You must also consider the capital gains tax (CGT) position (see Chapters 2 and 3). Taking the two taxes together, the 'best' gifts to make will tend to be the following:

- Cash gifts (always free of CGT) that qualify for an IHT exemption.
- Cash gifts that count as PETs (see page 57) for IHT purposes.
- Business assets that qualify for hold-over relief from CGT (see page 59) and count as PETs for IHT or qualify for business property relief.
- Other gifts that are exempt from IHT or that count as PETs and for which the CGT bill is relatively small due to unused CGT allowance, indexation allowance or CGT taper relief (see Chapter 3).

❝ Any IHT payable on your estate is a problem for your heirs, not you. ❞

For guidance on business property relief, see the **HM Revenue & Customs** website at **www.hmrc.gov.uk/cto/customerguide/page16.htm.**

127

Make tax-free lifetime gifts

Of particular importance for IHT purposes is your yearly tax-free exemption (see page 30), which lets you give away up to £3,000 each year without incurring any IHT liability. If you choose cash gifts, there will be no CGT either.

Another very useful gift that is free of IHT is normal expenditure out of income – this can be particularly handy when used in conjunction with an insurance policy (see page 27).

For tax purposes alone, it is not generally worth making, in your lifetime, a gift that would, in any case, be tax-free on your death – for example, a gift to charity. A safer course would be to retain the assets in case you need to draw on them and make the desired gift in your will.

Case Study Samir

Samir has a good income boosted by the return from a substantial portfolio of investments. From this income, he gives each of his three children £5,000 every Christmas. He has been doing this for a number of years and has kept meticulous records of the gifts, so there should be no problem convincing HM Revenue & Customs that these are normal expenditure out of his income. The gifts mount up, so that over a period of ten years, Samir will have given away £150,000 in total, completely free of IHT.

Give assets whose value will rise

If your aim is to reduce the value of your estate by the time you die, then it makes sense to give away assets whose value you expect to increase. In that way the increase will accrue to the recipient of the gift and will be outside your estate.

Make loans

One way to 'freeze' the value of part of your estate is to make an interest-free loan to someone and leave him or her to keep the proceeds from investing the loan. A condition of the loan would normally be that it is repayable on demand. From your point of view, this is more secure than making an outright gift and can be a useful arrangement if you are unsure whether or not you will need the money back at some time in the future.

Of course, there is little point demanding repayment of a loan if the borrower simply does not have the money available to repay you. An even more secure route would be to make the loan indirectly by giving it to a discretionary trust and naming the intended recipient as a potential beneficiary under the trust.

Consider lifetime gifts to a trust

The holy grail of all inheritance planning is to be able to give assets away tax-efficiently but still have access to them if later you find you need them after all. In general this is not possible because of the gift-with-reservation rules (see Chapter 4).

128

However, although *you* cannot be a beneficiary or potential beneficiary of a trust you set up without the assets you put into it counting as a gift with reservation, your husband, wife or civil partner can benefit. The fact of their being a beneficiary of the trust does not trigger the gift-with-reservation rules, provided that you yourself in no way benefit from your spouse's (or civil partner's) interest in the trust.

A further exception to the gift-with-reservation rules is that if you retain a reversionary interest (see page 80) in a trust to which you have given assets, the gift does not count as one with reservation.

But bear in mind:

- Since the April 2006 tax changes, whatever type of trust you use, the gift will almost certainly count as a taxable gift for IHT. There will be no immediate tax bill provided the gift is within your tax-free limit (£300,000 in 2007–8), but you'll need to survive seven years to ensure that the gift has no effect on tax on your estate, and
- The fact of your husband, wife or civil partner benefiting from the trust makes it a 'settlor-interested trust' (see page 88) for the purpose of the income tax and CGT rules. This will tend to make this type of arrangement unattractive.

Generation skipping

If you yourself inherit money or assets that are surplus to your needs, you might consider passing them on straight away to your children or grandchildren – this is a practice known as 'generation-skipping'. The transfer can often be made tax-efficiently through a 'deed of variation' (see page 201) or possibly a 'disclaimer' (see page 199).

If you inherit money or assets that are surplus to your needs, you might consider 'generation skipping'.

Case Study Tinuke

When Tinuke's mother died, she left an estate worth £280,000 to her daughter, made up of a property, cash, unit trusts and other investments. But Tinuke, by then aged 58, was already well settled with her own home and a good income from her career as an academic. Tinuke thought it over for a year or so and then decided she would rather that her grandchildren had the inheritance to use later towards their education.

Tinuke could just have given the money and investments to the grandchildren, in which case the gift would be a PET for IHT purposes and she would have had a CGT bill of around £12,000 on the gift of the non-cash assets.

Instead, Tinuke chose to have a deed of variation drawn up so that the gifts to the grandchildren were treated, for both IHT and CGT purposes, as if they had been made by Tinuke's mother in her will. Tinuke decided to get a solicitor to draw up the deed and this cost her about £600, but she saved £12,000 CGT. In addition, because there was no PET from Tinuke to her grandchildren, there are no tax implications if Tinuke dies within seven years.

Inheritance planning

129

USING LIFE INSURANCE

There are three straightforward ways in which life insurance can be a useful inheritance planning tool:

- Covering the potential tax bill on a PET.
- Making a gift that builds up outside your estate.
- Covering an expected tax bill on your estate.

These are discussed in turn below. All rely on making use of two factors:

- **Tax-free gifts**. Taking out insurance for the benefit of someone else means that the premiums count as gifts. You can ensure that there is no possibility of IHT on these premiums if you make sure they count as tax-free gifts. The most commonly used exemptions are to make the premiums as normal expenditure out of your income (see page 27) or to ensure that they fall within your yearly tax-free exemption of £3,000 (see page 30).
- **Trust status**. If the proceeds of an insurance policy are payable to you, the payout will be added to your estate when you die, which will increase the size of your estate and will cause delay before your beneficiaries have access to the payout. Therefore, it is important that the policy proceeds are paid direct to the intended beneficiary. You make sure this happens by 'writing' the insurance policy 'in trust', which means that the policy is held in trust for the benefit of whomever you name and the proceeds

are the property of that person rather than of you or your estate. Insurance companies will generally write a policy in trust for you at no extra charge (since they are able, in most cases, to use standard documents).

The cost of insurance increases with the likelihood of the insurance company having to pay out. So, if you are in poor health or very old, buying life insurance may be very expensive.

Potentially exempt transfers and insurance

If you make a gift that counts as a PET, you may want to be absolutely sure that any IHT bill that subsequently arises could be paid. (Similarly, you might want to ensure that any extra tax on a chargeable gift arising on death could be paid.) One way of ensuring this would be to take out a 'term insurance' policy.

Term insurance pays out if you die within a specified time – in this case, seven years; should you survive the specified period, it pays out nothing. Since the liability for IHT on a PET decreases as the years go by, the cover you need can also reduce – in other words, you want 'decreasing term insurance'.

PET insurance could be purchased by either the person making the gift or the person receiving it. If the giver buys the insurance it should be written in trust to pay out to the recipient in the event of the giver's death. The premiums the giver pays for the insurance count as a gift from the giver to the recipient but can be tax-free gifts if, say, they come within

130

the giver's £3,000 annual allowance or count as normal expenditure out of income. If the insurance is purchased by the recipient, the insurance is not a gift so there is no IHT implication.

Reducing the size of your estate

You could use life insurance to build up a gift that does not count as part of your estate. For example, you might use the full £3,000 yearly tax-free exemption to pay the premiums for an investment-type life insurance policy (such as an endowment or whole-life policy) that will pay out to the recipient either:

- After a specified period, in which case, you need an **endowment policy**, or
- When you die, in which case, you need a **whole-life policy**.

In choosing this strategy, you will need to weigh it against alternative strategies: for example, setting up a trust that could invest in a wide range of assets. The 'up-front' costs of setting up your own trust will be higher but the ongoing costs might work out to be less than for a life insurance policy. If you have relatively small sums to give, the insurance route would be more appropriate.

You can use personal stakeholder pension schemes in a similar way by making regular contributions to a scheme for someone else (see page 103). The charges for stakeholder schemes are capped at 1.5 per cent of the amount in the pension fund for the first ten years and 1 per cent thereafter.

Jargon buster

Decreasing term insurance Type of term insurance where the sum to be paid out on death decreases as the policy term progresses

Endowment policy Type of life insurance policy that runs for a specified term (often at least ten years). It pays out if you die within the term, but also pays out a cash sum at the end of the term. The amount it pays out will usually depend on the performance of an underlying fund of investments

Level term insurance policy Type of term insurance where the sum to be paid out on death stays at the same level throughout the policy term

Term insurance policy Type of life insurance that provides protection only and no investment. It pays out a pre-set sum if you die within a specified term but nothing if you survive

Whole-life policy Type of insurance that runs until the date you die. Because eventual death is a certainty, the policy must inevitably pay out at some time and so it builds up a cash value. The value is usually linked to an underlying fund of investments and tends to increase the longer you have the policy. Often, you can get a return from the policy by cashing it in during your lifetime (though the pay-out may be very poor in the early years)

131

Paying inheritance tax when you die

You could take out a whole-life policy to provide a lump sum to meet an expected IHT bill on your estate.

In essence, this is no different from using insurance as a way of making a gift on death, as already discussed, but the factors to consider are slightly different: you could save in your own investment fund (either within your estate or within a trust) to meet a potential IHT bill but it would take time to build up the full amount needed. If you died in the meantime, your investment would be insufficient to cover the tax. Taking out a whole-life insurance policy removes that risk because (provided you have bought the appropriate level of cover) it would pay out the full amount needed whether you die sooner or later.

If you have made a PET and die within seven years, the PET will use up some of the tax-free slice available at the time of death. This could cause extra tax to be due on the estate. Therefore, in addition to a whole-life policy to cover the main tax on the estate, it may be worth taking out a seven-year **level term insurance** policy to cover the extra tax bill on the estate if you die within seven years of making a PET. This is quite separate from a decreasing term insurance policy to cover possible tax on the PET itself (see page 130).

GIFTS FROM THE DEATHBED

If, say, you are seriously ill and do not expect to live for long, you might make a gift in contemplation of your death – known as a *donatio mortis causa*. Such a gift does not take effect until your death and it lapses completely if you do not die after all (or if the recipient dies before you).

In this situation, should your intention be to make an outright gift to someone that is not conditional on your dying, it would be wise to set down your intention in writing – in, say, a signed letter to the recipient – to safeguard against the gift being mistakenly treated as a *donatio mortis causa* (and thus being treated as part of your estate if you survive).

A further point to watch out for is that a gift that is made by cheque is not made until the cheque has been cleared against the giver's account. If death takes place before then, the gift would become invalid.

❝ A gift that is made by cheque is not made until the cheque has been cleared. ❞

132

Anti-avoidance rules

Complicated tax planning will not necessarily save you tax. In an ideal world, you would be able to make tax-efficient lifetime gifts to reduce the eventual tax on death but in the meantime continue either to have the use of the assets you give away or to get an income from them.

Not surprisingly, the tax authorities do not recognise this as a genuine gift. As described in Chapter 4, if you give something away but continue to benefit from it, you fall foul of the IHT gift-with-reservation rules. These work by continuing to include the value of the gift as part of your estate either until you cease to benefit or until you die, whichever happens first.

A variety of complicated schemes have been marketed that aim to exploit legitimate loopholes in the legislation that let you both reduce the size of your estate and continue to receive an income from the gifted assets. Many are now caught by the pre-owned asset tax (see Chapter 4) and the Revenue has made clear its intention to attack and close down new tax-planning schemes if it deems they are unfairly exploiting loopholes in the law (see Chapter 1).

Complex schemes have traditionally been the preserve of the seriously rich, but have become attractive to many more people in recent years because of the dramatic rise in house values. Chapter 10 outlines the strategies – albeit limited – that might help you to avoid or reduce inheritance tax on your estate if your home is your main asset and it is taking you above the IHT tax-free limit.

Do bear in mind, though, that IHT on your estate becomes payable only at your death. If that is likely to be many years ahead, circumstances might have changed – for example, although it is tempting to think that house prices will always keep on rising, this might not be the case. As the 'baby boom' generation inherits housing from their parents and, if government policies to increase the housing stock are successful, it could be that house price rises will become much more modest. This could mean a home which now only just tips into the IHT bracket might slip out again in future. Therefore think carefully before committing yourself to any complex IHT planning.

 If you are attracted to complicated tax planning, always get professional advice, for example, from a member of the Society of Trust and Estate Practitioners (STEP).

133

Using long-term care plans

Needing long-term care in later life can quickly eat away any wealth you have built up. Long-term care plans can limit the damage.

If you need care in later life, it could be very expensive. On average, a care home easily costs around £400 to £500 a week (up to £26,000 a year) but you could pay substantially more than this.

HELP FROM THE STATE

If your capital comes to less than £21,000 (England and Northern Ireland), £20,000 (Scotland) or £21,500 (Wales) in 2006–7 and your income is low, the State will pay some or all of the costs for you if you need to move into a care home. If your capital is greater than this, you will have to pay out of your own pocket until your capital has been run down to this level.

If your husband, wife or other dependant would be left at home, the value of your house should not be included in the assessment of how much capital you own. But, if you had been living alone, your home would normally count as part of your capital and might have to be sold to cover the care fees.

A long-term care plan can help you protect at least part of your capital.

How a long-term care plan could help

There are two types of long-term care plan you can consider:

- **Long-term care insurance**. You buy this in advance and it pays out a regular sum towards the cost of care if required in future. Long-term care insurance is not well developed in the UK and there are very few policies to choose from.
- **Immediate care plan**. You buy this at the time you need care with a single lump sum. The lump sum buys an annuity that pays out an income for the rest of your life. Provided the income is paid direct to the care provider, it is tax-free.

Long-term care plans are costly and buying them makes a large dent in your assets. But you can view this as damage-limitation, because you are swapping the uncertainty of large expenses for an indefinite period for a known cost.

For a more detailed look at long-term care plans, see *Be Your Own Financial Adviser*, available from Which? Books.

134

Making a will

It's estimated that seven out of ten people do not have an up-to-date will. Without one, it's unlikely the wealth you leave will be passed on in the way you had hoped and you could unnecessarily be leaving a handsome legacy to HM Revenue & Customs.

Why your will matters

None of us likes to think about death, but failing to write a will can leave a mass of problems for your survivors.

WHAT ARE THE PROBLEMS?

A will is a legal document that says how your possessions (your estate) are to be dealt with when you die. Even if your estate is small and your intentions regarding it extremely simple, you should still make a will. If you do not, a number of problems can arise, for example:

- Your survivors may waste time trying to find out whether or not you did write a will; it may take them a long time to trace all your possessions; and they may have to spend time and money tracing relatives.

- If there is no will, it may take longer and cost more to 'prove' the estate (an administrative process that has to be completed before your estate can be 'distributed' – that is, handed on – to your heirs).

- Without a will, your next of kin (often a wife, husband or civil partner) will usually be appointed to sort out your affairs. At the time of bereavement, he or she might prefer not to take on this role and you may, in any case, have friends or relatives who would be more suited to the task.

- The law will dictate how your estate is passed on and this may not coincide with your wishes.

- The law may require that various trusts are set up. The terms of these trusts may be overly restrictive and, especially where small sums are involved, unnecessarily large expenses may be incurred.

- Your heirs may have to pay IHT (or more tax) than would have been the case had you used your will to pass on your possessions tax-efficiently (see Chapter 9).

Jargon buster

Administrators The name given to your personal representatives if you have not made a will. They will distribute your estate in accordance with the law

Beneficiary A person or organisation left something under a will

Executors The name given to your personal representatives if you have made a will. They will try to ensure that the instructions in your will are carried out

Personal representative The person, people or organisation that sees that your estate is distributed following your death

Testator/testatrix The man or woman whose will it is. You must be aged 18 or over (and of sound mind) to make a valid will

Apart from avoiding these problems and ensuring that your possessions are given away as you would choose, a will can be used for other purposes too: you can appoint guardians to care for young children; and you can express your preferences about funeral arrangements and any wishes about the use of your body for medical purposes after death.

❝ Even if your estate is small and your intentions regarding it extremely simple, you should still make a will. If you do not, a number of problems can arise. ❞

Will facts and figures

- Although most people living as unmarried couples realise their partner will not automatically inherit from them, only 23 per cent have made a will.
- Over half of married people incorrectly believe their husband or wife would inherit everything even without a will. The figure is higher still (71 per cent) for civil partners.
- Nearly two-thirds of parents have not made a will, so are missing a straightforward way to ensure that their children are financially provided for and guardians appointed.

Scotland and Northern Ireland

The rules relating to wills and intestacy in Scotland and Northern Ireland differ in a number of respects from the rules for England and Wales. The rules described in the bulk of this chapter apply to England and Wales. For the differences in Scotland and Northern Ireland, see pages 145-6.

Dying without a will

If you die without making a will ('intestate'), the law dictates how your estate will be passed on.

The law aims, in the first instance, to protect your immediate family – husband, wife, civil partner and children. People who are not formally part of your family – for example, an unmarried partner – have no automatic rights under the intestacy laws (though they might still have a claim against your estate – see page 156).

Giving priority to your spouse and children might coincide with your wishes but, even if it did, the intestacy rules still might not result in your estate being used as you had expected or would have wished.

The intestacy laws assume that all your possessions could be sold by your personal representative to convert your whole estate into cash, which would then be distributed according to the rules described on pages 139–42. In practice, the possessions would not necessarily be sold and could be passed on intact, but problems can arise where there is a large possession – for example, the family home – if it needs to be split between two or more beneficiaries.

A welcome measure under the intestacy rules is that where part or all of your estate would pass to your spouse or civil partner, this will only happen if he or she survives you by at least 28 days. This 'survivorship provision' (which is also

a common device used in wills) makes sure that, in cases where you and your spouse or civil partner die within a short time of one another (for example, as a result of a road traffic accident), the relatives of each of you benefit from your respective estates rather than everything going to the relatives of the second to die.

A person under 18 (12 in Scotland) cannot make a valid will, so the estate of a child who dies – including any assets held under a bare trust for the child – will always be subject to the intestacy rules.

When you make a will, it should cover all your assets. But, if you fail to say how part of your estate is to be used, that part will be subject to the intestacy rules, even though the rest of your estate is disposed of in accordance with the will. This is called 'partial intestacy'.

Joint assets

The intestacy rules do not apply to joint assets where you hold them under a 'joint tenancy' (see page 147) with one or more other owners. Your share of such assets would pass automatically to the surviving co-owner(s).

WHAT THE INTESTACY RULES SAY

Without a will, the law decides who will inherit from you and gives preference to your husband, wife, civil partner and children.

If you are survived by a spouse or civil partner and no children

Your husband, wife or civil partner is entitled to all your personal chattels (meaning your personal possessions, such as clothes, furniture, jewellery and private cars). If your estate is valued at £200,000 or less, your husband, wife or civil partner also inherits the whole estate.

If your estate is valued at more than £200,000, your spouse or civil partner gets the whole lot, provided you had no living parents or brothers or sisters at the time of your death. If you are survived by parents, brothers or sisters, your spouse or civil partner is entitled to a fixed sum of £200,000 (plus interest at a set rate from the date of death until the date the payment is made) plus half of whatever remains. The remainder goes to your parents or, if they are dead, to your brothers and sisters. If a brother or sister has died, their children (if any) inherit in their place.

The £200,000 limit was set in 1993. In 2005, the government consulted on increasing the limit to £650,000 but, at the time of writing in December 2006, still no change had been made.

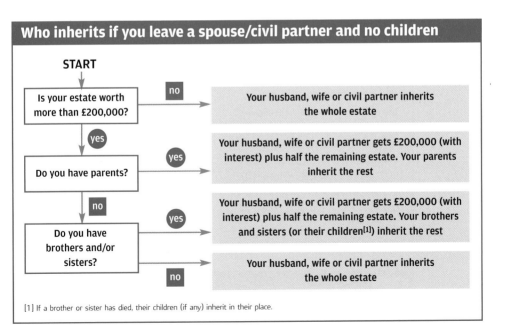

Who inherits if you leave a spouse/civil partner and no children

START

Is your estate worth more than £200,000? — no → Your husband, wife or civil partner inherits the whole estate

yes ↓

Do you have parents? — yes → Your husband, wife or civil partner gets £200,000 (with interest) plus half the remaining estate. Your parents inherit the rest

no ↓

Do you have brothers and/or sisters? — yes → Your husband, wife or civil partner gets £200,000 (with interest) plus half the remaining estate. Your brothers and sisters (or their children[1]) inherit the rest

no → Your husband, wife or civil partner inherits the whole estate

[1] If a brother or sister has died, their children (if any) inherit in their place.

139

If you are survived by children but no husband, wife or civil partner

If you leave children, but no husband, wife or civil partner, the inheritance position is simple: your children share your estate equally.

If you are survived by a husband, wife or civil partner and children

If, as well as children, you are survived by a husband, wife or civil partner, he or she is entitled to all your chattels. And, if your estate is valued at £125,000 or less, he or she also inherits the whole of that.

Jargon buster

Children For the purpose of the intestacy rules, 'children' includes offspring from your most recent marriage, any previous marriages, adopted and illegitimate children. But it does not include stepchildren, so even if you are married and regardless of whether you have always treated your partner's children from an earlier relationship as your own, your stepchildren will not inherit from you unless you make a will

If your estate is valued at more than £125,000, your husband, wife or civil partner receives a fixed sum of £125,000 (plus interest at a set rate from the date of death until the date payment is made) and a life interest in half of the remaining estate. A life interest gives him or her the right to the income from that part of the estate (or use of it in the case of, say, a house) but he or she cannot touch the capital. (Note that the husband, wife or civil partner can decide to take an appropriately calculated lump sum from the estate in place of a life interest – if you are in this situation, ask whoever is administering the estate to work out how much lump sum you would get before you make your decision.)

The rest of the estate passes to your children to be shared equally between them. If any child of yours has died, their children (if any) inherit in their place. They also become entitled to the capital bearing the life interest when your husband, wife or civil partner dies. Children can inherit capital outright only once they reach the age of 18, so they have an income entitlement up to that age.

The £125,000 limit was set in 1993. In 2005, the government consulted on raising the limit to £350,000. But, at the time of writing in December 2006, no change had yet been made.

 The government department with responsibility for advising the government on the intestacy limits is the Department for Constitutional Affairs, www.dca.gov.uk.

140

Who inherits if you leave children

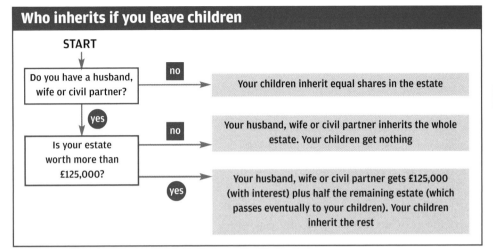

START

Do you have a husband, wife or civil partner? — **no** → Your children inherit equal shares in the estate

yes ↓

Is your estate worth more than £125,000? — **no** → Your husband, wife or civil partner inherits the whole estate. Your children get nothing

yes → Your husband, wife or civil partner gets £125,000 (with interest) plus half the remaining estate (which passes eventually to your children). Your children inherit the rest

Making a will

Case Study Alan

Alan died leaving an estate valued at £250,000. Of this amount £200,000 represented his half-share in the family home (which he and his wife, Julia, owned as tenants in common – see page 147). However, he had made no will. Under the intestacy rules Julia and his only child inherited the estate in the following shares:

Julia's share	
Capital: fixed sum	£125,000
plus interest	£3,090
Total capital	£128,090

Remaining estate
£250,000 – £128,090 = £121,910
So Julia also gets income/use from half of £121,910 i.e. — £60,955

Child's share	
Capital now	£60,955
Capital to be set aside for future (Julia has life interest)	£60,955

Unfortunately, Julia's outright inheritance of £128,090 and interest in a further £60,955 come to less than the value of the family home. In order to comply with the intestacy rules requiring capital of £121,910 in total to be set aside for the child, part of the family home must be held in trust for the child.

141

If you are survived by no near-relatives

If you leave no husband, wife or civil partner and no children, the intestacy rules rank your heirs in the order in which they will inherit your estate (see the chart, below).

If you have no relatives who are eligible to inherit, your estate passes to the Crown in *bona vacantia* (which literally means 'unclaimed goods'). The Crown may make ex gratia payments if your dependants or distant relatives make an application to it. It is important to realise that such claimants have no right to receive anything – payments are at the discretion of the Crown. Applicants who are most likely to succeed include the following:

- Someone who had a long, close association with you: for example, an unmarried partner or someone who lived with you as a child.
- Someone whom you clearly intended to benefit under a will that was invalid for some reason.

Who inherits if you leave no near relatives

[1] If a brother or sister has died before you, their children (if any) inherit in their place. If you have no full brothers or sisters, any half-brothers or half-sisters will share the estate instead.
[2] If any uncle or aunt has died before you, their children (if any) inherit in their place. If you have no full uncles or aunts, any half-uncles or half-aunts will share the estate instead.

142

PROBLEMS CAUSED BY INTESTACY

The main problems of intestacy arise where you are survived by a partner (either married or not) and/or you have children. Unless you make a will, you cannot be certain that they will be adequately provided for in the event of your death.

Unmarried couples

If you are not married to your partner, he or she has no automatic right of inheritance in the event of your death. However, they will be able to claim a share of your estate under the Inheritance (Provision for Family and Dependants) Act 1975 if they lived with you as husband, wife or civil partner throughout the two years prior to your death. If that condition does not apply but if they can show that they were being partly or wholly maintained by you when you were alive, they may still be able to claim support from your estate.

In either case, a claim must usually be made within six months of permission being granted to distribute the estate. It will then be considered by the courts, which is generally a lengthy and often costly procedure.

Married or in a civil partnership

If you are married or in a civil partnership, there is a tendency to assume that your husband, wife or civil partner will automatically inherit everything. The foregoing sections have shown that this is by no means certain.

Even if you are happy for your husband, wife or civil partner and children to share your assets, the practical application of the intestacy rules may be very distressing to your survivors. Where the estate must be shared between your spouse or civil partner and children, or shared with other relatives, your husband, wife or civil partner has the right to claim the family home as part or all of his or her inheritance (provided he or she lived there with you prior to your death). If the home is worth more than the amount he or she is entitled to inherit, your husband, wife or civil partner can 'buy' the excess from the estate. But if they don't have sufficient resources to do this, the home may have to be sold so that the cash raised can be split as required by the intestacy provisions.

❝ If you are not married to your partner, he or she has no automatic right of inheritance. ❞

Children

Minors cannot inherit directly under the intestacy laws, so any assets passing to children under 18 (and unmarried) must be held in trust.

The trustees will be required to invest the assets in accordance with the Trustee Act 2000, assuming the law of England and Wales applies. This places a number of duties and constraints on the trustees, in particular regarding the way the trust

143

assets are invested. Fortunately, the Act gives the trustees very wide investment powers. But they may be required to obtain professional advice, which could be unduly costly if only a relatively small sum is involved. In Scotland and Northern Ireland, the more restrictive investment rules of the Trustee Investments Act 1961 apply. This could mean an unduly high proportion of the trust fund being held as deposits, gilts and other bonds, and the trustees will be required to get investment advice unless they stick to a narrow range of investments largely made up of National Savings & Investments products.

Assets continue to be held in trust until the child reaches age 18, at which point he or she takes over direct ownership of the assets. This might be earlier than you would have wished. In a will, you could require assets to be held in trust until a later age (though the trust may then have to pay IHT – see Chapter 5).

TAX AND INTESTACY

Although intestacy might mean your estate is not passed on as you would have wished, it does in fact impose a certain amount of tax-efficiency. This is because the rules require a share of your estate above the fixed amounts to be passed to people other than your husband, wife or civil partner, so using

> ## Case Study   Ted
>
> If Ted had got around to making a will, he would probably have left everything to his wife, Jackie. She would have inherited £400,000 inheritance-tax-free, but when she subsequently died there would have been a large bill on her estate.
>
> As it was, Ted died intestate in late April 2007. Jackie inherited his personal belongings, the first £200,000 of the estate (plus interest) and a life interest in a further £100,000. The remaining £100,000 went direct to their grown-up son, John. He will also have the reversionary interest in £100,000 on which Jackie has the life interest.
>
> The intestacy rules mean that Ted, by default, has used £100,000 of his tax-free limit which could save the family up to £40,000 tax that might otherwise have been payable if Jackie had inherited the money first and then passed it on her death to John.

up some or all of your IHT-free limit. This can save up to £120,000 IHT (in 2007–8) on the subsequent death of your husband, wife or civil partner.

See page 52 for the inheritance tax limits for recent years and up to 2009-10.

144

INTESTACY IN SCOTLAND

The law in Scotland works differently for those who die without making a will, as follows. The amounts stated apply from 1 June 2005 onwards. Lower amounts applied before that date:

- **If you were married with no children**. Your husband or wife has 'prior rights' to the family home (provided it is in Scotland) up to a value of £300,000, furniture and household effects up to £24,000 and a cash sum up to £75,000. He or she also has 'legal rights' to half the remaining 'moveable estate' (i.e. excluding land and buildings). See below for the remaining estate.
- **If you were married with children.** Your husband or wife has prior rights to the family home up to £300,000, furniture and effects up to £24,000 and a cash sum up to £42,000 plus legal rights to share one-third of the remaining moveable estate. The children also have legal rights to share one-third of the moveable estate between them. See below for the remaining estate.
- **If you had a civil partner and no children**. Your civil partner has legal rights to half your moveable estate.
- **If you had a civil partner and children**. Your civil partner has legal rights to one-third of your moveable estate. The children also have a legal right to share one-third of the moveable estate between them.
- **If you had children but no husband, wife or civil partner.** The children have

legal rights to half the moveable estate.

- **The remaining estate**. Whatever remains after meeting the prior rights, the legal rights and, in the case of partial intestacy, bequests under a will is known as 'the dead's part' and is distributed in the following order of priority:
  - children
  - if there are both parents and brothers and sisters, half the remainder goes to the parents, half to the brothers and sisters
  - brothers and sisters, if there are no parents
  - parents, if there are no brothers and sisters
  - husband or wife
  - uncles and aunts (or, if they have died, their children)
  - grandparents
  - brothers and sisters of grandparents (or, if they have died, their children)
  - remoter ancestors, going back one generation at a time
  - the Crown.

> « Your husband or wife has prior rights to the family home up to £300,000, furniture and household effects up to £24,000 and a cash sum up to £75,000. »

INTESTACY IN NORTHERN IRELAND

The law is also different in Northern Ireland for those who die without making a will:

- If you were married or in a civil partnership with no children. Your husband, wife or civil partner inherits all your personal effects plus the first £200,000 of your estate and half of any residue. The remainder passes to parent(s) or brother(s) and sister(s) if there are no parents still living. If there are no children, no parents and no brothers or sisters (or nephews or nieces), then your spouse inherits your whole estate.
- If you were married or in a civil partnership with children. Your husband, wife or civil partner inherits all your personal effects plus the first £125,000 of your estate plus half of any residue if there is one child, or one-third of the residue, if there are two or more children. The remainder of the estate passes to the child(ren) – in trust if they are aged under 18.
- If you had children but no husband, wife or civil partner. The estate is divided equally between the children.
- If you had no children and no husband, wife or civil partner. Your estate goes to your relatives, starting with parents but extending to very distant relatives if no closer ones survive you.

❝ Some solicitors advise that you need a formal, signed and witnessed deed in order to switch from a joint tenancy to a tenancy in common. In fact, that is not the case. ❞

146

Jointly owned assets

How you own assets affects inheritance both under intestacy and if you make a will.

You may well have property, bank accounts, savings accounts and investments that are jointly held by you and someone else, typically your husband, wife, civil partner or unmarried partner.

In England, Wales and Northern Ireland, there are two ways of holding assets jointly: under a 'joint tenancy' or as 'tenants in common'. These are legal terms that can apply to any type of asset and not just to the way you share a home (different arrangements apply in Scotland – see overleaf).

Under a joint tenancy, you and your spouse or civil partner both own the whole asset, you have identical interests in it, and you cannot sell or give away the asset without the agreement of the other person. In the event of one of you dying, the other automatically becomes the sole owner of the asset (though the deceased person's share still counts as part of his or her estate). This automatic passing on of your share of the asset overrides the intestacy rules or any contrary instructions in a will.

Under a tenancy in common, you and your spouse or civil partner both have the right to enjoy or use the whole asset, but you each have your own distinct share in the asset and the shares need not be equal. On your death, your share

of the asset does not automatically pass to your husband, wife or civil partner and you can leave it to anyone you choose. If you have not specified who is to inherit your share, it is passed on according to the intestacy rules.

❝ Under a tenancy in common you each have your own distinct share in the asset. ❞

CHANGING THE WAY YOU SHARE OWNERSHIP

Some solicitors advise that you need a formal, signed and witnessed deed in order to switch from a joint tenancy to a tenancy in common. In fact, that is not the case. The law simply requires that one joint owner gives the other notice in writing. The notice does not have to be in any particular form – a letter would do – nor do you have to use any particular words. But your intention must be clear. To make matters doubly clear, you might consider drawing up a joint statement that you both sign.

Switching from a tenancy in common to a joint tenancy does require a formal deed, which a solicitor can draw up for you.

147

JOINT ASSETS IN SCOTLAND

In Scotland, jointly owned assets are nearly always held as tenants in common – i.e. with each person owning a distinct share of the asset. However, if the owners have agreed on it, there can be a 'survivorship destination clause' written into the ownership documents. Like joint tenancy in the rest of Britain, the survivorship destination clause ensures that the share of a co-owner who dies automatically passes to the remaining owner(s) – even if the will stipulates that something different should happen. Note that the clause can only be cancelled with the consent of all the owners and it requires a formal deed which can be drawn up by a solicitor.

SHARED OWNERSHIP AND OTHER TAXES

For income tax and capital gains tax (CGT) purposes, you are taxed on your share of any income or gain in proportion to the way you share the investment or other asset with other people.

But there are special rules for husbands, wives and civil partners. For income tax, HMRC will first assume that any assets you hold jointly are held under a joint tenancy. This means that you will each be treated as receiving half of any income from the asset. If you want the income to be treated differently, you need to send your tax office a completed form 17 (see below) setting out how the income is to be shared between you.

The way the income is split for tax purposes must reflect your actual shares in the asset. You cannot just choose the most convenient income split if it does not match the real shares and you cannot choose one split for income tax purposes and another for CGT.

Joint bank and building society accounts are almost always held as joint tenants, so can only ever be held on a 50/50 basis, but of course there's nothing to stop you transferring cash to your husband, wife or civil partner so they can pay into an account in their own name. If, exceptionally, you do hold an account as tenants in common, you must send HMRC proof of this arrangement at the time you submit form 17.

In the case of other assets, such as shares and unit trusts, say, you do not need to send in proof with form 17 but, if requested to do so, you should be prepared to provide some proof. This might be, say, copies of application forms or documents you signed when you first acquired the asset.

 You can get form 17 from the HM Revenue & Customs website (www.hmrc.gov.uk) or your usual tax office or a local tax enquiry centre.

148

Making a will

You could draw up your own will but usually it is better to get professional help, which need not be expensive.

In many people's minds, making a will is inextricably linked with using a solicitor but this need not be so. Provided your personal circumstances are straightforward and you understand what you are doing, there is no reason why you should not write your own will. The main advantage of writing your own will is, of course, the saving in solicitors' fees. But a simple will, for example involving only personal (no business) assets in the UK, with everything left to your husband, wife or civil partner, need not cost much even if you do go to a professional.

If your affairs are more complex, you should be wary of the DIY route. A will, to fulfil its purpose, must record your intentions clearly and unambiguously and should include contingency plans to cover the possibility, for example, of a beneficiary dying before you. There are also various pitfalls to be avoided – some that would invalidate the will and leave your estate subject to the intestacy laws and others that would not invalidate the will but would interfere with the intentions expressed in it. For example, a valid will must be signed by two or more witnesses, who may not also be beneficiaries (or the husbands, wives or civil partners of beneficiaries) under the will; so, if you are leaving anything to your husband, wife or civil partner, say, do not ask him or her to be a witness – the will would be valid but your spouse or civil partner would not be allowed to inherit under it.

If your affairs are complicated – for example, you run your own business, you have been divorced or you have stepchildren – or you do not feel confident about your knowledge of the law relating to wills, you would be wise to employ a professional rather than trying to draw up a will yourself. Lawyers claim to make more money from sorting out defective DIY wills than from writing wills themselves.

❝ Lawyers claim to make more money sorting out defective wills than from writing wills themselves. ❞

For more information on making a will, see the *Which? Essential Guide* to *Wills and Probate*.

149

WHERE TO GET A WILL

Solicitors are the best choice for most people and are not necessarily expensive.

Solicitors

The traditional source of help drawing up a will is a solicitor. Most high-street firms can draw up a simple will – leaving, say, everything to your husband, wife or civil partner. The cost of a simple will typically starts around £75. If you and your spouse or civil partner draw up similar wills at the same time (often called 'reciprocal wills', 'mirror wills' or 'back-to-back wills'), you might get a special rate of, say, £120 the pair.

> **!** Solicitors must belong to a professional body - one of the Law Societies - that lays down strict rules of business conduct backed up by disciplinary procedures and ensures that you have access to the Law Society Consumer Complaints Service (which is monitored by an independent commissioner) if things go wrong.

Will Aid

Will Aid is a fundraising campaign that is run on a two-yearly cycle. It involves a number of leading UK charities and has the dual aim of raising money for these charities and encouraging people to write a will. For one month, you can visit participating solicitors and have a basic will drawn up for free, but you are encouraged to donate the fee you would otherwise have paid to the participating charities. The suggested donation is £75 for a single will, £110 for mirror wills and £40 for a codicil (an amendment). You can use the Gift Aid scheme (see Chapter 6) to boost your donation. The next Will Aid campaign is in November 2008.

But, according to a survey by *Which? magazine*, prices vary greatly. It found the price of a single will could be as high as £146 and the charge for a pair of mirror wills ranged up to £293. So be prepared to shop around. If your affairs are complicated, the charge will depend on the time the solicitor needs to devote to your case and so you should expect to pay more. Always check the expected price before going ahead.

 Solicitors must pass exams, go through rigorous post-graduate training and continue to update their skills through continuous professional development. But dealing with estates is a specialist area, so you may prefer to choose a member of the Society of Trust and Estate Practitioners (STEP).

150

Will-writing firms

Will-writing services are an alternative to a solicitor. These are often small firms working under a franchise or as agents of a larger company. Most work by gathering the necessary details from you and feeding these into a computer which produces your will.

Unlike solicitors, people running, or working for, will-writing firms are not required to have any formal legal qualifications, though they will probably have received some initial training and the computer software they are using will have been developed using legal experts. These firms may also use a solicitor to draw up complex wills.

In the past, problems have arisen with some of these services: a number of firms have gone bust and, in one case, it was found that a potentially large number of the wills written contained a flaw and might not be valid. However, the will-writers' industry has been developing over the years and now many practitioners voluntarily belong to one of the trade bodies operating in this area.

The Institute of Professional Willwriters (IPW) and The Society of Will Writers (SWW) aim to promote the professionalism of their members. Both the IPW and SWW are in the process of applying to have codes of practice approved by the Office of Fair Trading (OFT) under its Approved Codes of Practice Scheme. Under the scheme, the trade body has to draw up a rigorous code that goes beyond the mere legal requirements and to be able to show that its code is working, it is rigorously enforced and consumers are benefiting. If satisfied, the OFT allows members of the trade body to use an OFT logo.

Will-writers generally charge a flat fee for wills and tend to be a bit cheaper than solicitors. Not surprisingly, the wills tend to have a standardised format – if your affairs are complex, a solicitor will normally be the better choice.

Other will-writing services

A third source of will-writing is banks, building societies and life insurance companies. These offer a will-preparation service but some insist that you agree to them also acting as executors of the will (which is not generally a good idea – see below).

You have an interview with the bank, society or company either at their offices or in your home. The interviewer you

❝If your affairs are complex, a solicitor will normally be the better choice. ❞

The process of applying for approval under the Office of Fair Trading Approved Codes of Practice scheme is lengthy. To check a trade body's code has been accepted and whether it has members in your area, check the OFT's codes website at www.oft.gov.uk/codes.

151

meet is not usually the person who actually draws up the will. If a bank or building society writes the will and you have a complaint, you can go to the Financial Ombudsman Service (FOS). The FOS does not cover insurance companies drafting wills.

Many charities also offer will-writing services. It is essential that you make sure that the solicitor or other will-writer is acting for you alone and that you do not feel under any pressure to make a bequest to the charity in your will.

❝ A solicitor or will-writer might offer extras. Do not feel pressurised into taking up any of these services unless you want to. ❞

OTHER RELATED SERVICES

In addition to writing your will, a solicitor or other will-writing service might offer extras, such as storing your will, drawing up a 'living will' (also called an 'advance directive') or severing a joint tenancy to create a tenancy in common (see page 147). Do not feel pressurised into taking up any of these services unless you want to. Bear the following points in mind.

Will storage

Most important is that your executors will be able to find your will and can be confident that it is your most recent will. If you are known to have a family solicitor, storing your will with the firm could be a good idea. You do not necessarily have to pay anything for this – some firms will store your will free of charge (because they hope to be employed later in executing your will). If you do not have an ongoing relationship with a solicitor, that might not be the best place to store your will. Other options include a bank safe-deposit box or a safe or strong box at home. Whatever you decide, it is a good idea to give your executors a sealed copy of the will.

Living will

This typically sets out in advance your wishes regarding healthcare – especially refusal of medical treatment – if you become incapacitated by a terminal illness or degenerative disease. In general, medical practitioners are required to give whatever treatment they deem necessary but a patient has the right to refuse treatment. Clearly an unconscious patient cannot do this but refusal can still be effective even if it was given in advance of becoming unconscious. There has been much debate about the legal status

 To find a solicitor, contact the relevant Law Society for details of its members. See page 212.

152

in the UK of living wills, but it seems that, provided the document states your intentions clearly and reflects your informed decision, a living will is likely to be legally binding. A good place to store a living will would be with your medical records.

Severance of joint tenancy

As discussed on page 147, if you want to transfer ownership of something – such as your home – from a joint tenancy to a tenancy in common, you do not need a formal deed drawn up by a solicitor. If you do not feel confident about getting the detail right, however, you might prefer a solicitor to draw up a notice for you.

APPOINTING EXECUTORS

You have a choice when it comes to deciding who will sort out your affairs for you in accordance with your will: you can appoint a professional as your executor – e.g. a solicitor or your bank – or you can appoint friends or relatives. In general, professionals often charge more and if problems arise, such as long delays, the beneficiaries can do little because they do not themselves have a contract with the executor, so have little access to information and limited power to challenge the executor's actions. If, instead, you appoint relatives or friends, they always have the option of employing a solicitor direct if they need help.

You can choose anyone you like to act as executor (provided they are aged 18 or over or 16 or over in Scotland when they apply for probate) and it is common to appoint the main beneficiary. Normally, you should appoint at least two executors, just in case one dies before you or refuses to act. Make sure you ask the people concerned whether they would be willing to take on the role.

Bear in mind that being an executor is a demanding task. Your executors will need to locate your will and personal papers, track all your assets and establish their value, establish what gifts you have made during the last seven years, deal with debts and funeral expenses, trace and contact beneficiaries, handle paperwork, deliver an account to HM Revenue & Customs and ensure any tax is paid. As tax will depend not just on the estate you leave but also on gifts made within the seven years up to death, your executors will be expected actively to try to trace gifts. This may mean trawling through old bank and building society statements and making enquiries among family members. Make sure you choose someone who has the time, energy and confidence to deal with officials and form-filling.

You can make your executors' lives easier if you lodge a record of your assets, their location and any gifts you have made along with your will or personal papers.

❝ Being an executor is a demanding task. Make sure you choose someone who has the time, energy and confidence. ❞

153

REVIEWING YOUR WILL

You should not view making a will as a task once done to be forgotten. As your circumstances alter, so your will needs to be updated.

In some situations – for example, if you marry, remarry or form a civil partnership – any will made before the marriage or civil partnership will automatically be invalidated (unless it was a will made specifically in contemplation of the marriage or civil partnership). All bequests and references to your ex-husband, ex-wife or ex-civil partner are automatically revoked by divorce or the dissolution of a civil partnership and the appointment of your 'ex' as guardian of any children will be revoked, unless you have made clear that this is still your intention. In other respects, the rest of your will stands.

The same is not true of separation – the whole will including bequests to your spouse or civil partner is still valid; in that situation, you should review the terms of your will.

Other circumstances in which you might want to revise your will are the birth or adoption of a child or if you decide that you would like to leave a legacy to a charity. It is wise to read through your will every two years, say, as a matter of course, to check that it reflects your current wishes.

If you do decide to alter a will – even slightly – it is better to draw up a new will containing the revisions than to add an amendment (a 'codicil'). The trouble with codicils is that they can easily become detached from the will and lost.

Beware of stapling, clipping or pinning anything other than a codicil to a will. It is quite likely that any other note or document would be detached before the will was sent for probate and the marks left on the will might then raise doubts about whether there had been a codicil attached that has become lost. Enquiries into the non-existent codicil could delay proceedings.

A new will should always start with a clause revoking any previous wills; this automatically invalidates any earlier wills. Interestingly, if a will is not automatically revoked – by, say, a later will or marriage – the law requires that you physically destroy your will if it is to be revoked. Simply putting a cross through it and scribbling 'cancelled' or 'revoked' across it is not enough.

MAKING GIFTS IN YOUR WILL

In your will, you can give away anything you own. There are different types of gift. The distinction between them is important both for tax reasons (see Chapter 9) and because of the order in which they can be redirected to meet expenses and settle debts that you leave at the time of your death. The main types of gift are described as follows.

Specific gift

This can be a named or identifiable possession, such as a piece of furniture, an item of jewellery or a particular car. It may be a specific possession that you own at the time you write the will. If you later sell the item the beneficiary

154

who was to have received it will get nothing after all.

Alternatively, you might leave a more general type of specific gift. This would be the gift of a possession but not restricted to a specific item that you own at the time of drawing up the will. For example, you might give away 'the car I own at the time of my death', which would take into account the possibility that you might change your car from time to time.

A specific gift might be even more widely defined: for example, simply 'a car'. In this latter case, the executors of your will would have a duty to make sure that the beneficiary received a car – either one that you owned at the time of death or, if you had none, one bought specifically to fulfil the terms of the will – or, alternatively, the trustees would have to pay over an equivalent sum of money.

Legacies

A 'pecuniary legacy' is a particular type of specific gift that is a straightforward gift of money: for example, '£1,000 to my niece, Claire'.

A 'demonstrative legacy' can be either a general gift or a pecuniary legacy, which is to be paid from a specific fund: for example, 'a violin to be paid for out of my account with Barclays Bank' or '£1,000 from my account with the Nationwide'. If there was not enough money in the account, the shortfall would have to be met by using other assets in the estate.

On the whole, it is best to keep bequests of particular items or demonstrative gifts to a minimum.

Particularly where your will is made a long time before death, there can be many changes to your possessions and the accounts and investments you hold.

Your personal representative(s) have wide powers (called the power of appropriation) to use any part of your estate to satisfy legacies. For example, if you leave £1,000 to your niece, the executors could give, say, shares worth £1,000 rather than selling the shares and giving her the proceeds from the sale.

66 As your circumstances alter, so your will needs to be updated. 99

Residuary gift (the 'residue')

A will that assigned every part of your estate as a particular gift or legacy would be out of date almost immediately, because the value of your estate fluctuates even in the course of your daily transactions and will alter more widely during the course of time. Therefore, it is usual to leave whatever remains of your estate, after all your debts, expenses and various gifts as listed above have been paid, as a 'residuary gift' or 'residue'.

You may intend your residue to be a substantial gift or it may be a small amount with, say, the bulk of your estate given away through pecuniary gifts.

To meet debts and expenses, any intestate part of your estate will be used up first, followed by the residue.

GIFTS YOU DO NOT MAKE

By omission, your will can also express your intention not to leave anything (or only very little) to people who might have expected to inherit from you. However, if these people were dependent on you (or you had a partner who had lived with you for at least two years as husband, wife or civil partner without necessarily being dependent), they have the right to make a claim through the courts under the Inheritance (Provision for Family and Dependants) Act 1975 for reasonable provision out of your estate. If you have not made a will, dependants who do not benefit under the intestacy can also make a claim under this Act.

The main people who are entitled to make such a claim are as follows:

- Your husband, wife or civil partner
- A former husband, wife or civil partner, provided he or she has not remarried (and is not precluded from making a claim under the divorce or dissolution settlement)
- A child of yours (whether legitimate, illegitimate or adopted)
- A child of your family (i.e. a stepchild or foster child)
- An unmarried partner.

An application under the Act must usually be made within six months of the personal representatives being given permission to dispose of the estate, though the court can extend this time limit. The court decides whether or not the applicant is entitled to financial support from the estate and, if it decides in favour of the applicant, it can order the payment of either a lump sum or income (or both).

You might seek to anticipate and thwart such a claim by giving away as much of your estate as possible but this strategy will not work. The court has the power to revoke such gifts in order to ensure that enough funds are available to meet the needs of your surviving dependants.

You can include in your will a statement setting out your reasons for excluding your dependants and the court will take this into account. It would be worth seeking advice from a solicitor about the most effective wording to use.

In Scotland, you cannot disinherit your husband, wife, civil partner or children, who can claim their 'legal rights' to part of your estate.

Tax at the time of death

Although you might be most concerned with the total amount of tax due on your whole estate, it's important to bear in mind how the tax bill will be distributed among your heirs.

Taxes triggered by death

When you die, you are deemed to make a final gift of all your possessions just before death. The good news is that there is no capital gains tax (CGT) on your estate, but there might be IHT on both the estate and any gifts in the seven years before death.

NO CAPITAL GAINS TAX

Whatever you give away on death is completely free of CGT. For CGT purposes, your heirs take over your possessions at their value on the date of death. This completely wipes out even very substantial gains that may have built up during your lifetime.

Any gifts with reservation during your lifetime (see Chapter 4) are still treated as part of your estate for IHT so might cause IHT to be payable. But gifts with reservation are *not* part of your estate for CGT purposes so do not benefit from the wiping out of gains. From the CGT point of view, the gift is valid from the date in your lifetime when you originally gave it away, so any increase in its value since then has built up in the hands of the recipient (and could be taxable when they dispose of the asset). In a way, this means that tax may be levied twice on the same gain in the form of IHT on your estate and CGT in the recipient's hands.

Planning point

If your husband, wife or civil partner is terminally ill, this is naturally a distressing time for the family and inheritance planning is unlikely to be foremost in your thoughts. However, it does present a tax-planning opportunity that you and your partner might wish to consider if your partner is looking at putting his or her affairs in order. If you own assets whose value has increased over the time you have owned them and would trigger a big CGT bill if you sold them, consider giving them to your partner. Gifts between husbands, wives and civil partners do not trigger an immediate tax bill (see Chapter 2) and on their death, any capital gains would become tax-free. If your partner leaves the assets to you in his or her will, you would reacquire them at their higher, present value. However, your partner would be free to leave the assets to anyone else. Your gift would not be genuine (and would not work for CGT-planning purposes) if it was conditional on it being given back to you in your partner's will.

TAX ON GIFTS MADE BEFORE DEATH

Chapter 3 looked at the immediate tax position of gifts made during your lifetime. With potentially exempt transfers (PETs) there is no IHT to pay at the time of the gift but, if you die within seven years, the gift may become taxable. The effective rate of tax ranges from 8 per cent up to 40 per cent, depending on the time that has elapsed since you originally made the gift (see page 57).

Similarly, a chargeable transfer – on which IHT may have been paid at the time of the gift at the lower lifetime rate of 20 per cent – is reassessed and there may be further tax to pay if you die within seven years of making the gift (see page 52).

The reassessment of these earlier gifts and payment of any tax on them is entirely separate from the calculation of tax on your estate. However, if you made PETs within seven years of dying, the fact that they have been re-assessed as taxable gifts will increase your running total up to the time of death and that could create or increase an IHT bill on your estate (see the case study overleaf). Moreover, there is no taper relief (see page 57) on any extra tax payable on the estate due to the reassessment of PETs. This is a constant source of confusion but taper relief can apply only

to tax on the reassessed PETs themselves; taper relief has no impact whatsoever on extra tax on the estate.

❝ There is no taper relief on any extra tax payable on the estate due to PETs. ❞

TAX ON YOUR ESTATE

On your death, IHT is due on the value of your estate plus your running total of gifts made in the seven years before death if they come to more than the tax-free allowance. The tax-free allowance for 2007–8 is £300,000. This may seem a large sum, but the £300,000 limit can soon be swallowed up, especially if you own your own home. Your estate is made up of:

- The value of all your possessions at the time of death, including your home, car, personal belongings, cash and investments.
- Plus any gifts with reservation (see Chapter 4) that you made and any assets that you elected to be treated as if they were gifts with reservation in order to escape the pre-owned asset tax (see page 75).

 See page 52 for tax-free limits for earlier years and the years up to 2009-10.

159

- Plus the proceeds of any insurance policies, which are paid to your estate.
- Less your debts.
- Less reasonable funeral expenses (say, around £2,000 but could be more).

This total is called your 'free estate' and it is the amount that is available for giving away. For the purpose of calculating any IHT, you can deduct from the free estate any gifts made in your will that count as tax-free gifts (see page 123). But you must add all the PETs and other taxable gifts that you made in the seven years before death to find the relevant running total. If the running total comes to more than the tax-free slice, IHT at a rate of 40 per cent is payable.

Case Study Praveen

In addition to using his £3,000 a year tax-free exemption, Praveen made the following gifts in his lifetime:

- 30 May 2003   £20,000 to a grandchild (a PET)
- 21 November 2006   £100,000 to a discretionary trust (a taxable gift)

On 16 August 2007, Praveen died. He leaves an estate of £300,000. You might think his estate is fully covered by the tax-free limit (£300,000 in 2007–8) and no IHT would be due. But the estate is not looked at in isolation. It is considered as the last gift Praveen made in a running total of gifts over the seven years. The PET in May 2003, now reassessed as a taxable gift, uses up £20,000 of the limit. The gift to the discretionary trust in November 2006 uses a further £100,000. This leaves only £180,000 of the limit to set against the estate, on which tax of £48,000 is due.

Praveen's tax-free allowance £300,000

PET £20,000	Gift to trust £100,000	First £180,000 of estate	Remaining £120,000 of estate

Inheritance tax
= 40% x £120,000
= £48,000

160

Gifts in your will

If tax is due on your estate, who pays it depends on the types of gift that you leave.

If the value of your estate plus taxable gifts in the seven years before death comes to less than the tax-free allowance, making gifts under your will is fairly straightforward. Assuming that the estate is sufficiently large (after paying off debts and expenses), the recipients will receive the amounts that you specify in your will.

However, if there is IHT due on the estate, matters are not always so simple. To work out how much the recipients will actually receive, you need to know how tax will be allocated between the various gifts.

DIFFERENT TYPES OF GIFT

For IHT purposes, there are three types of gift that you can leave in a will:

- **Tax-free gifts** (see Chapter 2). There is no tax at all on these.
- **Gifts that bear their own tax**. With these, the amount you give is treated as a gross gift out of which the recipient must pay any tax due.
- **Free-of-tax gifts** (not to be confused with tax-free gifts). The recipient gets the amount you specify and any tax due is paid out of the residue of the estate.

In general, a specific gift under your will is automatically treated as a free-of-tax

gift unless it is tax-free or you have explicitly stated that the gift should bear its own tax. But, to avoid confusion, it is a good idea to state for every gift whether it is 'free-of-tax' or 'to bear its own tax'. Whatever is left of your estate after deducting specific gifts is called the residue, which can be tax-free or taxable. Any taxable part bears its own tax.

The fun starts when you try to calculate how much tax will be deducted from each gift and the residue. The calculations vary depending on the mix of gifts. The following sections describe the main possibilities. If you find the calculations that follow daunting, do not despair – you can always ask your solicitor or accountant to work them out. The important point to grasp is that tax can affect seemingly similar gifts in different ways.

Planning point

Beware of specifying that a gift of a thing - for example, a piece of jewellery, furniture, painting or other heirloom - should bear its own tax, unless you are confident that the recipient has other resources from which to pay the tax. Otherwise, the gift you have made may need to be sold in order to pay the tax due.

161

HOW DIFFERENT GIFTS ARE TAXED

How your bequests are taxed might seem unimportant but just a few seemingly trivial words in your will can have a big impact on the amount each of your heirs inherits.

If all your gifts are tax-free

This is the simplest case. As with lifetime gifts, some gifts from your estate are free of IHT, in particular: gifts of any amount to your husband or wife, gifts to charities, gifts of national heritage property, gifts to political parties and gifts to housing associations (see Chapter 2).

For example, you might make a gift to charity and leave the residue to your husband or wife. Since both types of gift are tax-free, there is no IHT at all.

❝ Just a few seemingly trivial words in your will can have a big impact on the amount that each of your heirs inherits. ❞

Case Study **Connie**

When Connie dies in October 2007, she leaves an estate made up as follows:

Cottage	£65,000
Personal possessions	£21,500
Cash in bank	£496
Investments	£331,204
Gross value of estate	£418,200
less various small debts	£500
less funeral expenses, administration costs, etc.	£2,700
Net value of 'free estate'	£415,000

Connie had made no gifts during the previous seven years. Since the value of the estate exceeds the tax-free limit, you might expect IHT to have been payable. In fact, it was not, because Connie used the whole of the 'free estate' to make tax-free gifts. She left a legacy of £100,000 to charity and the residue to her husband.

If all your specific gifts bear their own tax

The amount of tax on each gift is in proportion to the values of chargeable gifts. This is done by working out the tax due on the whole of the chargeable estate and then expressing this as a percentage of the chargeable estate – this gives you an 'effective' IHT rate. The effective rate is then applied to each gift that is to bear its own tax to find out the amount of tax due on the gift. It is the recipients who pay the tax.

Case Study   Jim

Jim dies in July 2007 leaving an estate of £550,000. He makes two specific gifts bearing their own tax: £150,000 to his friend Ben and £180,000 to his cousin Gerald. He leaves the residue to his wife. Jim made no PETs or chargeable transfers in the seven years before he died. The tax position is worked out as follows:

Tax position of the estate

Value of free estate	£550,000
less tax-free gifts (i.e. residue to his wife)	£220,000
Chargeable part of estate (£150,000 + £180,000)	£330,000
less tax-free limit	£300,000
	£30,000
Tax on £30,000 @ 40%	£12,000
Effective tax rate ([£12,000 / £330,000] x 100)	3.636%

Who gets what

Tax on Ben's gift of £150,000 @ 3.636%	£5,455
Net amount Ben receives	£144,545
Tax on Gerald's gift of £180,000 @ 3.636%	£6,545
Net amount Gerald receives	£173,455
Amount left to wife	£220,000

If all your specific gifts are free of tax

The main complication in this situation is that, when the estate pays the tax due (out of the residue), it is deemed to be making a gift of the tax as well. To take account of this, all the free-of-tax gifts must be 'grossed up', which simply means that you find the total that equals the amount of the actual gifts plus the tax on them. The tax is then deducted from the residue.

Case Study | Alec

Alec also dies in July 2007 leaving an estate of £550,000. He makes two specific gifts that are free of tax: £150,000 to his friend Douglas and £180,000 to his friend Annette. He leaves the residue to his wife. Alec made no PETs or chargeable transfers in the seven years before he died. The tax position is worked out as follows:

Step 1: Grossing up the gifts

Add together all free-of-tax gifts (£150,000 + £180,000)	£330,000
less tax-free limit	£300,000
	£30,000
gross up £30,000 at the 40% tax rate (i.e. divide by 1 − 0.4 = 0.6)	£50,000
The grossed-up value of the gifts is £50,000 + £300,000	£350,000

Step 2: Tax position of the estate

Value of estate	£550,000
less tax-free part of the estate (£550,000 − £350,000)	£200,000
Chargeable estate	£350,000
less tax-free limit	£300,000
	£50,000
Tax on £50,000 @ 40%	£20,000

Step 3: Who gets what

Net amount Douglas receives	£150,000
Net amount Annette receives	£180,000
Amount left to wife (£550,000 − £150,000 − £180,000 − £20,000)	£200,000

If you leave free-of-tax and other taxable gifts

This is the most complex situation and is illustrated in the case study overleaf. Problems arise because the free-of-tax gifts must be grossed up by the IHT rate. The snag is that we do not know what IHT rate to use. The correct rate will depend on the amount of tax due on the whole chargeable estate which is made up of the gifts bearing their own tax as well as the free-of-tax gifts. But we cannot work out tax on the whole estate until we know the grossed-up value of the free-of-tax gifts. As you can see, we are in a circular trap.

The way out of the trap is to use a process called 'iteration'. Using iteration, you start with an estimate of the IHT rate – initially the death rate of 40 per cent – and repeat the calculation, each time using an improved estimate. You would have to go through the calculation several times to find the absolutely correct rate. But this involves a lot of work for only a small increase in the amount of tax collected and the tax authorities are happy to lose a bit of tax for the sake of making the calculations simpler. So, in practice, the tax authorities let you stop after two rounds by which stage the rate you are using is not perfect but ensures most of the tax due is collected.

You will need to do the same sort of calculation if, in addition to leaving free-of-tax gifts, you also divide the residue so that part is tax-free and part is taxable – this would be the position, for example, if you divided the residue between your children and your husband or wife. The taxable part of the residue is treated as if it is a gross gift bearing its own tax, so it does not need to be grossed up. See the case study on page 168.

❝ The tax authorities are happy to lose a bit of tax for the sake of making the calculations simpler. ❞

Leaving a mixture of gifts makes the sums complex. The examples on pages 166–9 show you how the sums work.

165

Case Study Alec

Suppose, in the example on page 164, of his estate worth £550,000, Alec left £150,000 free of tax to Douglas and £180,000 free of tax to Annette, as before, but also left a gift of £10,000 to bear its own tax to his daughter Judy. He leaves the residue to his wife. The tax position is as follows:

ROUND 1

Step 1: Grossing up the gifts

Add together all free-of-tax gifts (£150,000 + £180,000)	£330,000
less tax-free limit	£300,000
	£30,000
gross up at the 40% tax rate (i.e. divide by 1 – 0.4 = 0.6)	£50,000
The grossed-up value of the gifts is £50,000 + £300,000	£350,000

Step 2: Tax position of the estate

Value of estate	£550,000
less tax-free part of estate (£550,000 – £350,000 – £10,000)	£190,000
Chargeable estate	£360,000
less tax-free limit	£300,000
	£60,000
Tax on £60,000 @ 40%	£24,000
Notional rate of IHT ([£24,000 / £360,000] x 100)	6.667%

"Problems arise because the free-of-tax gifts must be grossed up by the IHT rate."

ROUND 2

Step 1: Re-grossing up the gifts using a better estimate

Total free-of-tax gifts	£330,000
gross up at the notional IHT rate	
(i.e. divide by [1 – 0.0667] = 0.9333)	
Re-grossed-up value of free-of-tax gifts	£353,584

Step 2: Revised tax position of the estate

Value of estate	£550,000
less tax-free part of estate	
(£550,000 – £353,584 – £10,000)	£186,416
New total for chargeable estate	£363,584
less tax-free limit	£300,000
	£63,584
Tax @ 40% on £63,584	£25,434
Final estate rate ([£25,434 / £363,584] x 100)	6.995%

Step 3: Who gets what

Tax on Judy's gift @ 6.995%	£700
Net amount Judy receives	£9,300
Net amount Douglas receives	£150,000
Net amount Annette receives	£180,000
Tax to be deducted from residue (£25,434 – £700)	£24,734
Amount left to wife	
(£550,000 – £150,000 – £180,000 – £10,000 – £24,734)	£185,266

See overleaf for an example where, in addition to a free-of-tax bequest, the residue is split between a tax-free and taxable gift.

167

Case Study Percy

Percy dies in October 2007 leaving an estate of £800,000. He makes a specific free-of-tax gift of £350,000 to his son, Harold, and leaves the residue equally to his wife and his daughter, Rose. Percy made no PETs or chargeable transfers in the seven years before he died. The tax position is worked out as follows:

ROUND 1

Step 1: Grossing up the gifts

Add together all free-of-tax gifts	£350,000
less tax-free limit	£300,000
	£50,000
gross up at 40% tax rate (i.e. divide by 1 − 0.4 = 0.6)	£83,333
The grossed-up value of the gift is £83,333 + £300,000	£383,333

Step 2: Tax position of the estate

Value of estate	£800,000
less tax-free part of the estate (£800,000 − £383,333 − [residue / 2])	£208,333
Chargeable estate	£591,667
less tax-free limit	£300,000
	£291,667
Tax on £291,667 @ 40%	£116,667
Notional rate of IHT ([£116,667 / £591,667] x 100)	19.718%

❝ Using iteration, you start with an estimate of the IHT rate – initially 40 per cent – and repeat the calculation, each time using an improved estimate. ❞

ROUND 2

Step 1: Re-grossing up the gifts

Free-of-tax gift	£350,000
gross up at the notional IHT rate	
(i.e. divide by [1 – 0.19718] = 0.80282)	
Re-grossed up value of free-of-tax gift	£435,963

Step 2: Revised tax position of the estate

Value of estate	£800,000
less tax-free part of estate	
(£800,000 – £435,963 – [residue / 2])	£182,018
New total for chargeable estate	£617,982
less tax-free limit	£300,000
	£317,982
Tax @ 40% on £317,982	£127,193
Final estate rate ([£127,193 / £617,982] x 100)	20.582%

Step 3: Who gets what

Harold receives	£350,000
Tax on Harold's legacy @ 20.582% of £435,963	
(to be borne by estate)	£89,730
Residue (£800,000 – £350,000 – £89,730)	£360,270
Wife receives (1/2 x £360,270)	£180,135
Tax on Rose's share of the residue	
@ 20.582% x £180,135	£37,075
Rose receives (£180,135 – £37,075)	£143,060

Successive charges relief

This relief is available to reduce a double tax charge where a beneficiary dies soon after inheriting.

If you left a substantial gift in your will to someone – for example, a son or daughter – who then died shortly after you, there could be two IHT bills on the same assets in a short space of time. To guard against this, a claim can be made for successive charges relief (also known as quick-succession relief).

This relief is available where the person inheriting the assets dies within

five years of the assets becoming part of that person's estate (even if the assets are then sold or given away before the recipient's death). The relief is deducted from the tax due on the estate of the second person to die, but at most the relief can reduce tax on the estate to zero. The relief is tapered: full relief is given if the recipient's death occurs within one year of the gift; a reduced rate applies if a longer time elapses (see the table, bottom left).

Successive charges relief is also available where the original gift was a lifetime gift and the recipient dies within five years. However, the amount of tax due, if any, on the original gift will not be known until seven years have passed since the gift was made, so there will be a delay before the amount of any relief can be calculated.

For successive charges relief to be available, there must be IHT on both the earlier gift and your estate. For example, if the earlier gift was tax-free or was covered by the giver's tax-free allowance, no tax would have been paid and so no relief can be claimed. This is the case even if the inclusion of the earlier gift in the estate of the second person to die is a major reason why IHT becomes due on the second death.

Successive charges relief

Years between first and second death	Tax relief on second death as a percentage of tax applicable to the original gift [1]
Up to 1	100
More than 1 and up to 2	80
More than 2 and up to 3	60
More than 3 and up to 4	40
More than 4 and up to 5	20
More than 5	no tax relief

[1] The percentage is multiplied by the formula:

$$\frac{G \times T}{E}$$

where G = the increase in value of the recipient's estate
E = the value of the earlier transfer or gift
T = the tax paid on the earlier transfer or gift

170

Case Study Joan

Sam's sister, Joan, died in May 2005, leaving him £50,000. Joan's whole estate was valued at £310,000. The tax-free limit then was £275,000 (see page 52) and so IHT of £14,000 was paid.

Sam dies in October 2007. He leaves an estate worth £480,000 to be shared by his two children. Tax on the estate would normally be 40% x (£480,000 – £300,000) = £72,000. But his personal representatives can claim successive charges relief in respect of the £50,000 he inherited. The inheritance was more than two but less than three years ago, so relief is due at 60 per cent. The relief equals:

$$\frac{\text{The increase in Sam's estate}}{\text{The value of Joan's estate}} \times \text{Tax on Joan's estate} \times 60\%$$

$$= \frac{£50,000}{£310,000} \times £14,000 \times 60\% = £1,355$$

The £1,355 relief is deducted from the IHT on Sam's estate, leaving a net IHT bill of £72,000 – £1,355 = £70,645

Case Study Ahmed

In February 2004 Ahmed gives his nephew, Jagdish, £30,000. The gift is a PET but Ahmed dies two years later. The PET is reassessed as a taxable gift and Jagdish pays £9,600 tax that then becomes due.

Tragically, Jagdish is killed in a car crash in November 2007. His estate of £450,000 passes to his partner. They were not married and IHT of £60,000 is charged on the estate. However, this is reduced by successive charges relief in respect of the gift from Ahmed. The gift was made more than three but less than four years before Jagdish's death so the successive charges relief percentage is 40 per cent. The relief is worked out as follows:

$$\frac{(£30,000 - £9,600)}{£30,000} \times £9,600 \times 40\% = £2,612$$

Tax on Jagdish's estate becomes £60,000 – £2,612 = £57,388.

Passing on your business

You may be able to arrange to pass on a business or farm without IHT taking a bite.

Handing on your business is a complex matter. There are many different ways of arranging the transfer, and which is appropriate for you will depend very much on your particular circumstances.

Business planning is outside the scope of this book and the aim of this section is just to draw to your attention to the fact that important reliefs against IHT may be available when you pass on a business.

BUSINESS PROPERTY RELIEF

If, on death, your business passes to someone else, your personal representatives may be able to claim 'business property relief' which will reduce the value of the transfer of the business for IHT purposes and thus reduce or eliminate any IHT otherwise payable. To be eligible, you must have been in business for at least two years. Only 'qualifying' business assets attract relief; these are assets that are either:

- Used wholly or mainly for the purpose of your business, or
- Are required for future use by the business.

Assuming you operate your business as a sole trader or as a partner in a partnership, business property relief will be given at the higher rate of 100 per cent – that is, it could completely eliminate an IHT charge.

Relief of 100 per cent is also available if you pass on a holding of shares in an unquoted company – which includes shares traded on the Alternative Investment Market (AIM).

A lower rate of business property relief – set at 50 per cent – is available to set against transfers of a controlling holding (i.e. 5 per cent or more) in a fully quoted company.

Business property relief is intended to take most handovers of family companies outside the IHT net. However, even 100 per cent relief will not necessarily entirely mitigate an IHT bill. In particular, you

Passing on your business or farm is a complicated area with a lot at stake, so get advice from your accountant and a solicitor.

172

should note that, if the business property is subject to a binding contract for sale, relief will not normally be given. This might be the case where, say, a partnership has arranged that the surviving partners will buy out the share of a partner who dies; the deceased partner's share of the business would not qualify for relief in this situation. This sort of problem can be avoided with some advance planning – for example, by giving surviving partners the option but not the obligation to buy – so it is very important that you get advice from an accountant or other tax adviser at the time you draw up the partnership agreement.

Most types of business can qualify for business property relief. The only exception is businesses whose sole or main activity is dealing in stocks, shares, land or various other investments. Letting out property does not normally count as a business and so does not usually qualify for business property relief.

Any IHT due after business property relief has been given can be paid by interest-free instalments over a period of ten years.

❝ Most types of business can qualify for relief. ❞

AGRICULTURAL PROPERTY RELIEF

Agricultural property relief – which is similar to business property relief – is available when a farm is handed on. The relief, which is given automatically and does not have to be claimed, is given against the agricultural value of the land and buildings. The equipment and stock do not qualify for agricultural property relief but they may qualify for business property relief. Note that the agricultural value of the farm may be lower than the market value if, say, the land has development value – the excess will not qualify for agricultural property relief, though it may be eligible for business property relief.

To qualify for agricultural property relief, you must either have occupied the farm, or a share of it, for the purpose of farming for at least two years, or you must have owned the farm, or a share in it, for at least seven years. If you farmed the land yourself, relief is given at the higher rate of 100 per cent. If you let the land to someone else to farm, relief is restricted to the lower rate of 50 per cent.

As with business property relief, agricultural property relief is also not available if the farm is subject to a binding contract for sale (see above).

Any IHT due after relief has been given can be paid by interest-free instalments over a period of ten years.

Telling the taxman

When you die, your personal representatives will be responsible for sorting out your estate.

Before your personal representatives can distribute any of your assets to your heirs, they must obtain probate (in England, Wales or Northern Ireland) or confirmation (in Scotland), which is proof of their right to dispose of the assets. Probate or confirmation is granted only after any IHT due has been paid (or in some cases partly paid) or your representatives have shown that no tax is due.

66 Probate or confirmation is granted only after any IHT due has been paid (or in some cases partly paid). 99

THE FORMS YOUR PERSONAL REPRESENTATIVES NEED

If no IHT is due and the estate counts as an 'excepted estate', your representatives will normally deliver a simplified account of the assets in your estate to the Probate Registry on form IHT205 (England or Wales), the Probate and Matrimonial Office on form IHT205 (Northern Ireland) or Sheriff's Court on form C1 (Scotland) (for contact details, see below). The relevant form will be included in the pack your personal representatives are sent on contacting the relevant probate registry, office or court or they can download it from the HM Revenue & Customs website.

For deaths on or after 6 April 2004, an excepted estate is one where all the following conditions are met:

- The person who died had their permanent home in the UK.
- The estate involves either no trusts or only one trust in which the deceased person had an interest in possession.

 For form IHT205, go to www.hmrc.gov.uk/cto; for the Probate and Matrimonial Office, go to www.courtsni.gov.uk; or for the Sheriff's Court, go to www.scotcourts.gov.uk. For phone numbers and addresses, see pages 210-13.

174

- No more than £100,000 of the estate is trust property.
- No more than £75,000 of the estate property is situated outside the UK.
- Any gifts in the seven years before death were of cash, chattels, quoted shares or securities, land or buildings and came to no more than £100,000. Gifts covered by the small gifts exemption, yearly tax-free limit, wedding gifts and normal expenditure out of income can be ignored but other tax-free gifts must be included.
- Any gifts of land and buildings within the seven years before death were outright gifts to another person (e.g. not gifts into a trust).
- The person who died had not made any gifts with reservation (see Chapter 4) or elected to have any transfers treated as if they had been gifts with reservation in order to escape the pre-owned assets tax (see page 70).

AND THE ESTATE IS EITHER

- **Small**. The gross value of the estate and gifts in the seven years before death does not exceed the IHT-free limit

OR

- **Exempt**. The gross value of the estate and gifts in the seven years before death does not exceed £1 million and the value of the estate, excluding

amounts passing tax-free to a spouse, civil partner or charity, comes to no more than the tax-free limit.

The relevant tax-free limit is normally the amount for the year in which death occurs but is the amount for the previous tax year if the death occurred between 6 April and 5 August inclusive and the representatives apply for probate by 5 August.

If the estate is not an excepted estate or if IHT is due, the personal representatives must complete a detailed account on form IHT200, which they can obtain from the HM Revenue & Customs and which is sent to the relevant HMRC Inheritance Tax office. The time limit for sending in form IHT200 is 12 months from the end of the month in which death occurred or, if later, within three months of the personal representatives starting to act.

" If the estate is not an excepted estate or if IHT is due, the personal representatives must complete a detailed account on form IHT200. "

For detailed information about the personal representatives' role and how to complete the forms involved, see the *Which? Essential Guide* to *Wills and Probate*.

PAYING THE TAX

Your personal representatives have six months from the end of the month in which death occurred within which to pay any IHT due – less if they want to get probate/confirmation granted sooner than this. The time limit for paying the tax is generally earlier than the time limit for delivering the IHT200 form and your personal representatives may find initially they have to base the tax bill on an estimated account. Once the account is finalised, they pay any extra tax due or claim a refund of any overpayment. Interest is charged on tax paid late and added to refunds.

Having to pay the tax before the grant of probate/confirmation throws up another problem. The personal representatives will not necessarily have any ready cash with which to pay the bill. Although in general assets cannot be released to the representatives before probate/confirmation, there is an exception that allows some types of asset to be released early specifically to pay the IHT under a scheme whereby the money due is transferred direct to HM Revenue & Customs. These assets are: most National Savings & Investments products, gilts and, where banks and building societies have signed up to the scheme, money held in bank and building society accounts. If there are no such assets available or they fall short of the amount of tax due, the personal representatives may need to take out a temporary loan to pay the tax.

Where tax is due in respect of land, buildings, shares that gave the deceased a controlling interest in a company (whether listed or unlisted) or certain unquoted shares, the personal representatives can apply to pay the tax in ten equal yearly instalments. Interest is charged on the amount outstanding.

HMRC can agree to accept heritage property in lieu of some or all of the IHT due. Eligible property includes pictures, prints, books, manuscripts, works of art and scientific objects, provided they are 'pre-eminent' for their national, scientific, historic or artistic interest. Buildings and land of outstanding scenic, historic or scientific interest and items associated with them are also eligible.

❝ The time limit for paying the tax is generally earlier than the time limit for delivering the IHT200 form. ❞

HM Revenue & Customs used to publish a range of free guides about IHT. These have now all been withdrawn and instead you can find guidance on the Revenue website at www.hmrc.gov.uk/cto/customerguide. If you do not have access to the website, contact the Probate and Inheritance Tax Helpline on 0845 3020 900.

176

Tax and your home

IHT planning is especially tricky if most of your wealth is tied up in your home. You can't save tax by giving away your home in your lifetime if you still need to live there. But there are some other options you could consider, including sharing your home and equity release schemes.

10

Basic planning

In essence, your home is no different from any other asset. Many of the planning points in earlier chapters apply equally to your home.

The bulk of this book applies to your home as much as to any other asset. However, because your home is both the place where you live and likely to be your most valuable possession, it is worth drawing together here some of the points you should bear in mind if you are contemplating making a gift of your home either as a lifetime gift or at the time of death.

WHO OWNS WHAT?

If you own your home jointly with someone else, it is important to think about how you own it. As discussed in Chapter 8, there are two forms of joint ownership (in England, Wales and Northern Ireland): joint tenancy and tenants in common.

If you own your own home as a joint tenant with someone else, you each have equal shares in the home and have identical rights to enjoy the whole home. On death, the share of the owner who dies passes automatically to the remaining co-owner(s). This is very simple and convenient and can be the best arrangement for married couples and other partners in stable relationships, especially if the value of their estates taken together is no more than the

tax-free limit for IHT (£300,000 in 2007–8).

However, owning the home as tenants in common gives you greater flexibility and better scope for tax planning. Tenants in common still have the right to enjoy the whole home but you each have distinct shares in the home which need not be equal and do not pass automatically to the other owner(s) on death. Instead, the share of the home is passed on in accordance with your will or, if you had not made a will, the rules of intestacy.

USING YOUR TAX-FREE LIMIT

Failing to use the tax-free limit when the first partner of a married couple or civil partnership dies can result in an unnecessarily large tax bill when the second dies (see Chapter 7).

With ownership of the home arranged as tenants in common, it becomes possible for each partner to arrange to use their tax-free limit by, for example, passing their share of the home on to their children instead of to their wife or husband. This can save IHT overall but is worth doing only if you can be sure that the surviving spouse will continue to have a secure home – for example, if the recipients give him or her the protection of a formal tenancy agreement (see below). Using a will trust (see Chapter 7) is a more complicated way of making sure the tax-free limit is used and the surviving partner is secure in the family home.

THE IMPORTANCE OF A WILL

Chapter 8 described the problems that can arise if you die intestate. These can be especially acute if your home is the main asset in your estate.

If you die without a will and you are survived by children or other relatives, your husband, wife or civil partner inherits outright only a certain part of your estate. He or she does have the right to opt to take his or her share of your estate in the form of the home rather than other assets. But what if that share of your estate is worth less than the home? The husband, wife or civil partner may well find that part of the home has to be put into trust for the benefit of young children, say, or that older offspring or more distant relatives insist on the sale of the home in order to release their own inheritance as cash.

The position of an unmarried partner is even worse. He or she may have no automatic right to share in your estate.

However, if he or she has been your partner throughout the two years up to death or has been financially dependent on you, he or she can apply to the courts under the Inheritance (Provision for Family and Dependants) Act 1975 (see page 156).

Therefore, if the home is jointly held as tenants in common, it is essential that you make a will specifying how your share of the home is to be passed on.

❝ If the home is jointly held as tenants in common, it is essential that you make a will specifying how your share of the home is to be passed on. ❞

If your spouse will need the protection of a tenancy agreement, get help from a solicitor in drawing up the will and making sure that the relevant safeguards are built into it.

179

Your home as a lifetime gift

It would be very tax-efficient if you could give away your home during your lifetime. The snag is: you also need somewhere to live.

YOUR ONLY OR MAIN HOME

If you expect your estate at death to exceed the tax-free limit, it would be convenient if you could give away your home now in your lifetime. Making a gift of your home to your children, say, would count as a potentially exempt transfer (PET). There would be no IHT to pay at the time you made the gift and, provided you survived seven years, no IHT at all. But if you give away your home, where do you intend to live? If you mean to stay in the home, the gift will not work for IHT purposes, because it will count as a gift with reservation (see Chapter 4). There are a couple of ways around this problem, though neither is very satisfactory.

First, you could share the home with the people to whom you give it. Provided you all live together and you bear your full share of the running costs of the home, the gift should not count as one with reservation. But, if the recipients subsequently move out, the gift will become a gift with reservation – so make sure you do not fall out!

The second solution relies on the caveat that a gift is not a gift with reservation if you give full consideration in money or money's worth for the use you continue to make of the gift. For example, you could give away your house but pay the full market rent to live there under a tenancy agreement or licence. Or you could buy a lease at the full market rate which lets you live in it for some specified period – for example, long enough to cover your expected remaining years, plus a few extra years to be on the safe side. Alternatively, you might offer your services as, for example, a housekeeper or gardener, provided the value of your work was equivalent to the market rent for the property you continue to occupy.

Other promising ideas tend to fall foul of the rules governing associated operations (see Chapter 1) or the pre-owned assets tax (see Chapter 4). Tax experts, from time to time, come up with other complicated schemes, but their legal status is often unclear and the Revenue is quick to lay a challenge.

The only satisfactory way of giving your home as a lifetime gift is if you genuinely do have somewhere else to

If you want to explore more complex ways to make a lifetime gift of your home, get professional advice from an accountant or other tax adviser.

180

live – for example, a retirement cottage or moving in with friends or relatives.

MORE THAN ONE HOME

Giving away a property is obviously more feasible if you have more than one home. But you need to take care that any continuing use you make of the property you have given away does not trigger the gift-with-reservation rules. The IHT legislation says that a gift with reservation occurs if the recipient of a gift does not enjoy the gifted assets 'virtually to the entire exclusion of the donor and of any benefit to him'. These words are not defined but the Revenue has provided some guidance on benefits you might still enjoy without triggering the reservation rules – see box, below.

CHANGE OF PLAN

Suppose your circumstances change and you move back into a home you had previously given away? This could trigger the gift-with-reservation rules. However, if you become unable to maintain yourself because of old age, infirmity or some other reason and your moving

back into your old home is a reasonable way for the recipient of the gift – who would have to be your relation or spouse – to provide care for you, the gift-with-reservation rule will not apply.

WATCH OUT FOR CAPITAL GAINS TAX

Giving away your home does not normally trigger a capital gains tax (CGT) bill, because any gain on your only or main home is generally exempt. In some situations, however, there could be a CGT bill. These arise where:

- You have lived away from home for a time.
- You have let out all or part of the home.
- Part of the home has been used exclusively for your work.
- The garden was greater than the normal size for a home of that type (usually taken to be greater than half a hectare).

If you give away a second home, CGT will normally be payable on the gift – see Chapter 3.

Benefits that should not trigger the gift-with-reservation rules

In relation to a home you have given away, they include:

- You stay in the home in the absence of the recipient for no more than two weeks a year.
- You go to stay in the home with the recipient but for no more than a month a year.
- You are invited to make social visits that do not include overnight stays, provided you visit

the recipient no more often than you would have done if the gift had not been made.

- You stay temporarily with the recipient for a special reason, such as while you or the recipient is convalescing or your home is being redecorated.
- You visit the home in order to babysit or for some other domestic reason.

181

Problems if you cohabit

If you share a home with, say, an unmarried partner, a sibling or your adult children, IHT on death might force the sale of your home. Planning ahead can help to avoid problems.

A husband, wife or civil partner inherits tax-free from their partner, so there is no problem passing the family home to the survivor. But a bequest to an unmarried partner, a brother, sister, child, friend or carer is a taxable bequest. If your estate is worth more than your tax-free limit, IHT will bite into the amount you leave them. This can cause a problem if your major asset is your home and that person shares it with you, because the home may have to be sold to raise the money to pay the tax.

The problem can arise both where a valuable property is jointly owned and where only one of the cohabitees owns the property.

POSSIBLE SOLUTIONS

If you or your cohabitee might have to sell up to pay an IHT bill when one of

Sisters challenge the law

Two sisters, Joyce and Sybil Burden, took a case to the European Court of Human Rights. The sisters, in their 80s, share and jointly own the family home which they inherited and where they have lived their whole lives. With rising house prices, the home is now worth £875,000. Although they have left their share of the home to each other, the hefty tax bill that would be due on the first death (up to £70,000 at 2007-8 rates) means that the surviving sister would have to sell the home to pay the tax.

The sisters claimed that their rights under article 14 of the Convention on Human Rights, which outlaws discrimination, were being violated, since married cohabitees or civil partners would not pay tax or be forced to sell their home.

In December 2006, the court agreed that married couples and civil partners were treated differently, but said the UK government *'cannot be criticised for pursuing, through its tax system, policies designed to promote marriage; nor can it be criticised for making available the fiscal advantages attendant on marriage to committed homosexual couples'*. It concluded that the different treatment under UK law is reasonable and justified and the sisters lost the case

182

you dies, there is only a limited range of options that you could consider.

Create a joint ownership

If you are the sole owner of a property that you share with one or more other people and you would like them to be able to carry on living in the home, an answer might be to give a share in the home to the other cohabitee(s). Points to bear in mind are:

- The gift will normally be a potentially exempt transfer (PET), so to be effective in saving tax you need to survive seven years after making the gift (see Chapter 3).
- You must not benefit from the part of the home you give away. If you do, the PET will fail and instead you will have made a gift with reservation that stays in your estate (see Chapter 4). In practice this means you must pay at least your full share of the running costs of the home or pay a market rent to your co-owner(s).
- There will be no CGT on the gift, provided the home is your only or main residence.
- If even your remaining share of the home is above your tax-free allowance, a problem may remain and you may want to consider insurance (see above right).
- Consider your own security should a co-owner die before you. Your security would be greatest if you owned the property as joint tenants (see page 147).

Take out whole-life insurance

Whether you are the sole owner of a property or own a valuable share, you could consider taking out whole-life insurance written in trust for your co-owner(s) to cover any IHT due on your death (see page 132). Other co-owners should consider doing the same to protect your security.

This solution is feasible if you are still reasonably young and fit. But if you are getting on in age and/or your health is poor, insurance could be prohibitively expensive.

Case Study Beth

Beth is the sole owner of a house worth about £380,000, which she shares with her adult daughter, Viv. Beth is retired and Viv is disabled. The family does not have much income and very few assets apart from the house. As it stands, if Beth dies, there would be an IHT bill of at least £32,000 to pay. Viv would then have to sell the home to pay the tax.

Beth decides to transfer a half share in the home to Viv. This reduces Beth's estate to around £190,000 which is now well within her tax-free limit (£300,000 in 2007-8) provided she survives seven years after making the gift so that it drops out of the running total of gifts up to the date of death. For the gift to work, it is essential that Beth does not benefit from the half of the home that she has given away, so she must pay at least half of all the costs associated with the home. Beth and Viv would be wise to keep records of how they split the bills, just in case they have to prove their case to HM Revenue & Customs at some time in the future.

183

Equity release schemes

These schemes let you raise money from your home while you still live there and, in the process, also reduce the value of your estate. But there is a price to pay.

WHAT ARE EQUITY RELEASE SCHEMES

Equity release schemes are a way of raising money from the capital you have tied up in your home. There are two main types of scheme:

- **Lifetime mortgage**. You take out a mortgage on your home. Usually this is a 'roll-up' loan which means you don't pay any interest on the mortgage during your lifetime. Instead, the interest is added to the outstanding loan, which is eventually repaid when you no longer need the home – usually on your death but possibly earlier if, say, you move permanently into long-term care.
- **Home reversion scheme**. You sell all or part of your home to a reversion company. You receive a lump sum now and retain the right to live in the home either rent-free or for a peppercorn amount for as long as you still need the home. The reversion company gets its money back from the sale of the home after you have died or, say, moved permanently into care.

In either case, schemes can be taken out for a single person or a couple. In the latter case, the right to remain in the home continues until the second of you dies or moves into care.

Equity release schemes were mainly designed to address the problems of older homeowners who are 'asset rich, cash poor' enabling them to raise extra income or cash from their home in order, say, to boost their income or pay for repairs to their home. But increasingly they are also being marketed as a way to mitigate IHT.

HOW AN EQUITY RELEASE SCHEME REDUCES INHERITANCE TAX

An equity release scheme reduces the value of your estate and so any potential IHT bill in two ways:

- First (but not particularly helpfully), you do not get full value for the part of your home you mortgage or sell (see the case study, opposite). So you get an instant depreciation in the value of your estate.
- Second, and more positively, the money released is yours to do with as you will. Provided you don't keep it, it ceases to be part of your estate. You could spend the money. You could use

184

it to make lifetime gifts. You could use it to buy an annuity to provide you with extra income for life. (The annuity ceases to be part of your estate at the time you die because the income stops on death.) But if you keep and invest the money raised, it will continue to be part of your estate, in which case the equity release scheme will not be particularly effective in saving IHT.

ARE EQUITY RELEASE SCHEMES VALUE FOR MONEY?

There is no easy answer to this question. It depends how much you value being able to have cash now either to spend or to give away while being able to remain in your home.

The only way to release the full value of the equity in your home is to sell it and move somewhere cheaper. There are sound reasons why an equity release scheme does not give you full value for the part of your home you give up.

In the case of a typical lifetime mortgage, you are not paying any interest during your lifetime. The unpaid interest is added to the outstanding loan, so you or your heirs will eventually have to pay back a lot more than just the original amount you borrowed. Because interest is then charged on the loan plus the interest already rolled up (a process called 'compounding'), the outstanding

Case Study Rosemary

Rosemary, aged 70, has an estate worth £580,000, but £460,000 of this is tied up in the value of her home. When she dies, Rosemary's whole estate will pass to her daughter, Claire. Based on today's values, there would be an IHT bill of 40% x (£580,000 – £300,000) = £112,000.

Rosemary has been thinking about taking out a home reversion scheme. The one she has in mind would give her a lump sum of £101,500 if she sold half her home. This would reduce her estate as follows:

- An immediate reduction of £230,000 (half of the home which is sold) less £101,500 (the lump sum raised) = £128,500. This represents the loss of value through using equity release and the charges for the scheme.
- Provided Rosemary spends or gives away the £101,500 raised, her estate will eventually be reduced by the full £230,000 (at today's values).

IHT on Rosemary's estate would be reduced to 40% x (£580,000 – £230,000 – £300,000) = £20,000. This is a tax saving of £92,000. But Rosemary has effectively lost £128,500 of her estate in order to make this tax saving.

 For a more detailed look at equity release schemes, see *The Which? Guide to Money in Retirement*. See also www.which.co.uk for advice on equity release.

185

loan increases at an alarming rate – see the table, below. You should always check that any lifetime mortgage has a 'no-negative-equity guarantee'. This means that the outstanding loan will never grow to more than the value of the home, so you and your heirs should never owe more than your home is worth.

With a home reversion scheme, the company buying your home or a share of it for cash today will normally have to wait many years until it gets its cash back. The company estimates how long that will be by looking at the average life expectancy of someone of your age and gender and then estimates how much it

Roll-up lifetime mortgage: an example

Years since plan taken out	Rate of interest (fixed for duration of plan)		
	5%	7%	9%
Initial loan	£50,000	£50,000	£50,000
1	£52,500	£53,500	£54,500
2	£55,125	£57,245	£59,405
3	£57,881	£61,252	£64,751
4	£60,775	£65,540	£70,579
5	£63,814	£70,128	£76,931
6	£67,005	£75,037	£83,855
7	£70,355	£80,289	£91,402
8	£73,873	£85,909	£99,628
9	£77,566	£91,923	£108,595
10	£81,445	£98,358	£118,368
11	£85,517	£105,243	£129,021
12	£89,793	£112,610	£140,633
13	£94,282	£120,492	£153,290
14	£98,997	£128,927	£167,086
15	£103,946	£137,952	£182,124
16	£109,144	£147,608	£198,515
17	£114,601	£157,941	£216,382
18	£120,331	£168,997	£235,856
19	£126,348	£180,826	£257,083
20	£132,665	£193,484	£280,221

could have earned on the money by investing it elsewhere rather than in you. That cost to the company is then passed on to you as a reduction in the cash sum. The older you are when you take out the plan, the more you will get back for any given value of your home that you sell. For example, a 70-year-old might get say £45,000 for every £100,000 of home they sell, while a 80-year-old might get £55,000.

The reversion company buys a percentage of your home (100 per cent if you sell your whole home) and takes that percentage of the sale proceeds when the home is eventually sold. This means the reversion company, not you or your heirs, benefits from any rise in the value of the part of the home you sold. If house prices rise steeply, the reversion company will make a handsome profit. But the reversion company also takes the risk of a much lower profit if house prices rise only modestly or even a loss if house prices fall.

Case Study **Chris**

Chris takes out a lifetime mortgage of £100,000 against his £350,000 home. The mortgage is at a fixed rate of 7 per cent a year with the interest being rolled up and added to the outstanding loan. Chris lives another 12 years. When he dies, the outstanding loan plus interest has nearly tripled to £225,220. But his house has also increased in value to just over £700,000. Once the mortgage has been repaid, £474,780 still remains to be added to Chris' estate and passed on to his heirs after IHT has been paid.

"Consider discussing the scheme with family members so they understand the implications for the amount they might inherit. "

Planning point

Before entering into an equity release scheme, make sure you fully understand that you will not get the full value of the part of your home you give up. Consider discussing the scheme with family members and any others who would stand to inherit from you, so that they too understand the implications for the amount they might eventually inherit.

Case Study **Rosemary**

Rosemary sells 50 per cent of her home when it is worth £460,000. This raises a lump sum of £101,500. When Rosemary dies nine years later, her home is worth £777,000. The reversion company takes 50 per cent of this, in other words £388,500. The remaining £388,500 remains in Rosemary's estate to be passed on to her daughter after IHT has been paid.

187

COSTS AND RISKS OF EQUITY RELEASE

Apart from the value-for-money question, there are a number of other aspects to equity release schemes that you should consider carefully when weighing up whether this is the right course of action for you.

The suitability of you and your property

Equity release schemes are designed for people from, say age 60 or 65 upwards. The amount of money you can raise increases with your age at the time you take out the scheme.

To be eligible, you need to have a suitable property. Some providers will not offer schemes on flats. Most will not accept sheltered housing. Usually your property will need to be worth at least a minimum amount and be free of any existing mortgage.

Valuation

With a home reversion scheme, it is crucial that it is based on a fair valuation of your home's current value. Make sure the valuation is carried out by a valuer who is independent of the reversion company.

Immediate and ongoing costs

Make sure you understand all the costs involved in the scheme you choose.

There is likely to be an arrangement fee for a lifetime mortgage – say, several hundred pounds. This can be added to the outstanding loan, but interest will then be charged on it, so you might prefer to pay the fee out of the money you raise.

With a reversion scheme, there is usually an arrangement fee of, say 1 to 2 per cent. Check whether this is a percentage of the value of the home you sell or a percentage of the amount of money you raise. Do not pay the fee upfront – it should be deducted from the money you raise after the deal is complete.

There will be a survey and valuation fee. The scheme provider might offer to reimburse this on completion of the deal.

With a lifetime mortgage, you may have legal costs. With a home reversion scheme, it is essential that you get advice from a solicitor who is acting for you rather than the reversion company, so allow for these costs.

You will be expected to keep the property insured and well maintained. The maintenance requirements may be particularly detailed with a reversion scheme. So you need to allow for these ongoing costs. Get your solicitor to check the terms of the tenancy agreement carefully.

Check whether there are charges if you want to end the scheme early.

Effect on state benefits

Be wary of taking out an equity release scheme if you are receiving any means-tested state benefits, such as pension credit.

Your eligibility for benefits and the amount you get depends on your income and capital, so raising money from an equity release scheme will affect this.

The scheme provider or any independent financial adviser you are using should be able to advise on this or refer you to an appropriate alternative source of information. Your local Citzens' Advice Bureau can estimate the likely effect for you.

Possible effect on tax liability

If you are aged 65 or over and receiving extra personal allowance (age allowance) against income tax, using an equity release scheme to provide income could result in some allowance being lost and a rise in your tax bill.

This is not a problem where you use a scheme to raise a lump sum. In practice, even schemes providing 'income' are often structured to provide a series of capital sums that are not within the scope of income tax. But bear in mind that if you invest a lump sum, interest or other income from the investment could boost your taxable income and reduce your age allowance.

Moving home

Check what happens if, after taking out the scheme, you want to move house. Can you transfer the scheme to another property? What restrictions are there on the type of property you can choose? (Bear in mind that sheltered housing is not usually eligible.)

Sharing your home

If you are married or living with a partner, to ensure their security if you were to die or move into care first, you should take out a joint equity release scheme. This will ensure that the home does not need to be sold until neither of you needs it any more.

Normally, there is no security of tenure for someone who moves in with you after you have taken the scheme out. And you will need to check with the lifetime mortgage or reversion scheme provider whether they will allow someone to move

Planning point

Equity release schemes that you take out at **arm's length** with a commercial company are outside the scope of the pre-owned assets tax (POAT) – see Chapter 4. But if, on or after 7 March 2005, you arrange your own scheme with, say, a relative or friend, you might be caught. However, bear in mind that a yearly benefit of less than £5,000 does not trigger a POAT bill – see the case study on page 76.

Jargon buster

Arm's length The term HM Revenue & Customs use to describe the sort of commercial deal you would make with someone you did not know on the open market as opposed to a special arrangement you might strike with a friend or family member

To find details of your local Citizens' Advice Bureau go to: www.citizensadvice.org.uk.

189

in with you. This could be an issue if, say, you decide to marry late in life or you want a family member or carer to move in with you as you get older.

Family expectations

Whatever your reason for taking out an equity release scheme – to save IHT, to raise income – it will reduce the value of the estate you leave on death. It is generally advisable to discuss this with family members and any others who expect to inherit from you.

HOW EQUITY RELEASE SCHEMES ARE REGULATED

Lifetime mortgages are regulated by the Financial Services Authority (FSA). This means that providers and advisers have to be solvent, competent and abide by good business standards. They must also provide you with adequate information before you buy, including a Key Facts document which sets out important information, such as charges and your obligations, in a clear format that makes it easy to compare one scheme with another. Provided you deal with a firm authorised by the FSA, you are covered by proper complaints procedures if things go wrong, including the independent Financial Ombudsman Service. If you lose money because of bad advice about a lifetime mortgage, you may be eligible for

compensation from the Financial Services Compensation Scheme.

Home reversion schemes will become regulated by the FSA from 6 April 2007 onwards, when similar rules to those for lifetime mortgages will apply.

Many equity release providers belong voluntarily to a trade body called Safe Home Income Plans which sets standards for its members.

Before taking out an equity release scheme, make sure you get advice from a solicitor acting for you and an independent financial adviser (IFA). Make sure the provider and IFA are regulated by the Financial Services Authority (FSA) by checking the FSA Register.

To find a solicitor and IFA, see the contact details on page 212. To check whether a firm is authorised by the FSA, see www.fsa.gov.uk/register or call 0845 606 1234.

190

Receiving an inheritance

Inheritance planning does not end when the giver dies. A person receiving an inheritance can also take steps to claim or alter a bequest and possibly minimise the tax paid.

Your rights as a beneficiary

Being named as a beneficiary under a will should be good news but matters do not always run smoothly.

FINDING OUT ABOUT AN INHERITANCE

One of the jobs of the personal representatives appointed to sort out a will is to trace the beneficiaries named in the will. In many cases, the personal representatives are also the beneficiaries or close relatives of them, so there is no problem letting the beneficiaries know about their inheritance.

If you are named in a will but the personal representatives don't know how to contact you, they must make reasonable searches to try to find you. This might include, for example, checking the deceased's address books, questioning relatives and friends of the deceased, and employing a specialist tracing agency.

In other cases, the will might not name you specifically but perhaps you are one of a class of beneficiaries and the personal representatives might not be aware that you exist.

In general, if you were to turn up after the estate had been distributed with a valid claim to an inheritance, the personal representatives would be personally liable to meet your claim. But the representatives can protect themselves by publishing appropriate notices calling for beneficiaries and creditors of the estate to make themselves known. The notices must appear in *The London Gazette* (England and Wales), *The Belfast Gazette* (Northern Ireland) or *The Edinburgh Gazette* (Scotland), a newspaper local to the area where any land in the estate is situated, and any other local or national newspapers that are appropriate given the circumstances. They must give a period of at least two months during which you should get in touch – the notice will give contact details of the personal representatives or their solicitors.

❝ One of the jobs of the personal representatives is to trace the beneficiaries. ❞

 Pursuing a claim on an estate after it has been distributed is a difficult area and you will need the help of a solicitor.

192

The Gazette

The London Gazette, The Belfast Gazette and *The Edinburgh Gazette* are the UK's official newspapers of record. When the law requires information to be published – for example, regarding companies or insolvencies – generally, wherever else it is published, a notice must also appear in the appropriate edition of *The Gazette*. So this is the official publication in which personal representatives, if they wish to protect themselves, must advertise for claimants to an estate. You can view the deceased notices placed in *The Gazette* free on the Gazettes website (see box, below).

If you have not come forward within the notice period, you no longer have a claim against the personal representatives. However, you do still have the right to pursue your claim to the inheritance and, if it is valid, have the right to try to recover the assets or money involved from the other beneficiaries. If they are sympathetic, they might agree to share the estate with you. If not, you would need to pursue your case through the courts. Even if your claim is established, it might not be possible for you to inherit if the assets or money has already been dissipated and can no longer be traced.

> **❝ In the worst event, after all the expenses and debts, there might not be anything left. ❞**

PROBLEMS WITH EXECUTORS

While an estate is in administration, the money and property belong to the personal representatives, not the beneficiaries. The personal representatives are not even holding the estate property on trust for the beneficiaries, because until the estate is sorted out, the representatives cannot know how much of the property will have to be used to meet bills and pay off other creditors. In the worst event, after all the expenses and debts, there might not be anything left to share out among the beneficiaries. So, even if you have been left a specific item in a will – 'the ormolu clock', 'my ruby necklace', 'my stamp collection' – you have no right to it until the representatives release it.

To check the notices in *The London Gazette, The Belfast Gazette* or *The Edinburgh Gazette*, see www.gazettes-online.co.uk.

Receiving an inheritance

193

However, beneficiaries could object if the personal representatives sold a named asset unnecessarily.

Personal representatives are allowed a period of at least a year in which to sort out the estate. Some estates are complex and will take much longer – sometimes many years. But at some point, you might feel the representatives are dragging their heels and should speed up.

Other problems might be the impression that the representatives are taking too much from the estate in expenses or charges, selling assets at less than their full value, or worse.

In general, if you are dissatisfied with the way the representatives are handling their job, your only course of action is to apply to a court for help. A court has a range of possible remedies, for example, requiring personal representatives to seek court approval before selling or distributing assets and replacing or removing personal representatives. You could take out a personal action against a representative for redress or against people you believe have wrongly received assets from the estate.

"If you are dissatisfied with the way the representatives are handling the job, your only course of action is to apply to a court for help. "

194

Tax and your inheritance

Inheritance tax, capital gains tax and income tax can all have a bearing on the amount you eventually receive.

INHERITANCE TAX

There is no IHT as such on anything you receive under a will. But the estate may have had to pay tax and, depending on the type of bequest you receive, this tax may have reduced the amount you receive as described in Chapter 9.

If you have been left a bequest that bears its own tax (see page 161), a share of the estate tax bill will have been deducted from any cash sum before it is handed over to you. Such gifts are more problematic if you are left an asset rather than money. In that case, you will have to find cash from elsewhere to pay the tax or, alternatively, sell the asset in order to raise the cash to pay the tax.

Even if there is a delay before the estate is distributed, if you inherit an asset (rather than cash), you are treated as having acquired it on the date of death of the deceased at the open market value of the item on that date. This will be the same as the value of the asset as shown in the estate accounts.

CAPITAL GAINS TAX

For capital gains tax (CGT) purposes, you are also treated as having acquired an asset that you inherit on the date of death of the deceased at its open market value on that date.

If the personal representatives sell assets and pay out cash to the beneficiaries, it is the estate not the beneficiaries that is liable for any CGT on the sale due to any increase in value since the date of death. Of course, any tax paid by the estate reduces the amount left to be distributed to the beneficiaries. Usually tax bills will reduce the residue of the estate, but if the residue has been used up, other bequests could be affected.

INCOME TAX

There is no income tax on the actual inheritance you get but there could be tax on any income earned by the estate after the date of death and before the estate is wound up. The personal representatives are responsible for income tax on any income received by the estate during administration. They pay tax at the basic rate, savings rate or 10 per cent dividend rate, depending on the type of income.

If any of the income is paid out to you either during administration or when the estate is finally distributed, it counts as part of your income for the year in which you receive it. With the income from a UK estate, you get a tax credit for the tax already paid at the basic, savings or

195

Jargon buster

Grossed-up amount When related to income tax, this means the net amount of income you receive plus the tax credit or tax already deducted. For example, if you receive £80 from which £20 tax at the savings rate has already been deducted, the grossed-up amount is £80 + £20 = £100. If you are a higher-rate taxpayer, you would have extra tax to pay equal to 20% x £100 = £20

in a tax return including the supplement headed 'Trusts etc'. The notes accompanying the supplement give details of what tax might be due and what to enter on the return.

If you were left cash in the will and there is a delay before the cash is paid out to you, you might receive interest from the personal representatives in recognition of the delay. Usually, you will receive the interest without any tax deducted and, if you are a taxpayer, you must declare this income and pay any tax due.

dividend rate. If you are a non-taxpayer or pay tax at the starting rate, you can reclaim all or part of the basic-rate or savings-rate tax credit. You cannot reclaim any of the tax credit with dividends. If you are a higher-rate taxpayer, you have extra tax to pay on the grossed-up amount of the income. (**Grossing up** means you add the tax credit to the income you received to find the before-tax amount.)

The personal representatives should give you a completed certificate R185 (Estate income) setting out the amount of each type of income, the amount of each tax credit and whether it is reclaimable.

The position is more complicated if you receive income from a foreign estate. In that case, there might be UK income tax to pay. You will need to fill

Case Study Sanjay

Sanjay's uncle died in December 2006 and his cousin, Rajiv, is dealing with the estate. In 2007-8, Rajiv paid out some of the cash from the estate, which included interest that had been earned since the date of death. Sanjay received interest of £80 together with a tax credit of £20 representing tax at the savings rate of 20 per cent, which had already been deducted. Sanjay is a higher-rate taxpayer, so he has extra tax to pay. The grossed-up interest is £80 + £20 = £100. Tax at the higher rate would be 40% x £100 = £40 but Sanjay can set the tax credit against this, leaving £20 tax to pay.

Cash or assets?

Sometimes you are offered a choice about the form in which you receive an inheritance. Tax treatment is a factor to take into account in making your decision. (If you are not offered a choice but have a preference, you could ask the administrators of the estate if they would be willing to hand over your inheritance in your preferred form.)

YOUR OPTIONS

Typically, an estate will be made up of a mix of cash (bank accounts, savings accounts, and so on) and assets (for example, property, furniture, other personal possessions, shares). Unless you have been left specific items, the personal representatives might offer you the choice of taking your inheritance in the form of cash or some of the assets in the estate.

Substituting assets instead is an example of 'appropriation' (see page 155). The choice has tax implications:

- **Cash**. The personal representatives sell assets in order to pay you cash. They are liable for any CGT on an increase in the value of the assets since the date of death and the tax is a bill paid using the estate's funds. The personal representatives are liable for CGT at a single 40 per cent rate but have a tax-free allowance set at half the rate an individual gets (£4,600 in 2007–8).

If the asset has fallen in price since death, the representatives could set the loss against other gains made by the estate or alternatively use the lower value to adjust the IHT bill due on the estate, in either case saving tax at 40 per cent. You, as beneficiary, have no personal CGT liability and cannot make use of any losses, because you receive cash.

- **Assets**. The personal representatives pass the assets direct to you. You are treated as having acquired the assets on the date of death. Therefore you become liable for any CGT on any increase in value since the date of death, but only when you eventually sell the assets. You may be liable for CGT at 10, 20 or 40 per cent, depending on your personal tax position and have an annual tax-free allowance of £9,200 in 2007–8 (see Chapter 3). If the assets fall in value, you can use the loss in the normal way as set out in Chapter 3.

197

Often the residue of an estate is to be divided among several beneficiaries. If some of the beneficiaries opt for cash and others for assets, the personal representatives need to value the assets in order to ensure that each beneficiary gets a correct share. If the price of the assets changes frequently – as in the case of, say, shares – the personal representatives will set a fixed day on which the valuation will take place.

66 Opting for cash could be worthwhile if you want to spend some of your inheritance straight away, maybe paying off your mortgage or other debts. 99

DECIDING WHAT TO DO

These are the points to consider when weighing up what to do.

Taking cash

Opting for cash could be worthwhile if you want to spend some of your inheritance straight away, maybe paying off your mortgage or other debts.

If you would want to invest your inheritance, taking cash might still be sensible if you expect asset prices to fall or the assets are not the sort you would want to invest in.

Taking the assets to sell immediately

Weigh up the tax position. Would the CGT you would have to pay be less than the amount the personal representatives would pay? Or, if the assets are standing at a loss, could you claim more tax relief than the representatives?

Also consider the sale price and any selling costs. Could the personal representatives get a better deal than you? This might be the case if, say, the assets are shares and the personal representatives would be selling in bulk.

Would you benefit from any tax or cost savings made by the personal representatives (because you get a share of the residue) or would the benefit go to other beneficiaries under the will?

Taking the assets to keep

This could be a good idea if the assets are suitable for you and the type you would choose to hang on to. If the assets are investments, you need to consider how they fit in with your overall financial planning and whether they match the level of risk you are comfortable taking.

To explore financial planning more generally, see *Be Your Own Financial Adviser* from *Which? Books*.

198

Renouncing your inheritance

You cannot be forced to accept an inheritance if you don't want it. If you simply disclaim the bequest, you have no control over what happens to it. If you want to redirect the gift to someone else, a deed of variation may be more appropriate.

DISCLAIMING YOUR INHERITANCE

Disclaiming an inheritance means you simply give up your rights to receive it. A disclaimer must cover the whole of the item concerned, not part of it. For example, if you were left 'the money in my current account' you could not give up just half of it and take the rest. But where you have been left more than one distinct item, you could disclaim one but accept another.

You cannot disclaim an inheritance if you have already accepted it or started to benefit from it (by, for example, receiving interest from it).

The inheritance effect of the disclaimer is as if your right to inherit had not existed. So, if you disclaim part of the residue of an estate, the intestacy rules take over for the part you disclaimed. Where you were left a specific bequest or legacy, whatever you disclaim becomes part of the residue and is passed on in accordance with the rest of the will or, if there was no will, the intestacy provisions.

Tax and disclaimers

As far as IHT and CGT go, the disclaimer is treated as if it had been made by the deceased person provided certain conditions are met in which case there are no tax implications for you. (There could be IHT implications for the estate if, say, the bequest to you was a tax-free gift but will now pass as a taxable gift to someone else.) The conditions are:

- The disclaimer is made within two years of the date of death.
- It is made in writing, and
- You do not receive anything in return for making the disclaimer.

If you do not meet these conditions, you are treated as having made a lifetime gift

To disclaim an inheritance, contact the personal representatives in writing within two years of the death.

199

(usually a PET) to whoever gets the item instead and as having made a disposal for CGT purposes (see Chapter 3).

> ❗ There is no special income tax treatment if you disclaim an inheritance or alter it using a deed of variation. This does not normally cause a problem but, if the effect of your disclaimer or variation is that the bequest passes instead to your unmarried child under age 18, HM Revenue & Customs is likely to argue that the anti-avoidance legislation covering parental gifts to children applies (see page 70). This would mean that, if the inheritance produced more than £100 a year income for the child, that income would be taxed as yours.

❝ With a variation, you decide how the inheritance should be redirected. A variation must be agreed by all the original beneficiaries. ❞

USING A DEED OF VARIATION

Another way of changing your inheritance is to draw up a 'variation'. In effect, this is like re-writing the will of the person who died, though technically you are not varying the will itself just the gifts made under it.

Unlike a disclaimer, with a variation you decide how the inheritance should be redirected. It can be used not simply to renounce an inheritance (say, in favour of your grandchildren instead of you) but to alter its form (for example, changing an outright gift to a life interest) or save tax (for example, ensuring that the deceased person's tax-free limit is used).

Other differences from a disclaimer are that a variation can be made even if you have already started to benefit and it can affect just part of the inheritance if that's what you want.

A variation must be agreed by all the original beneficiaries affected by the will or that part of it which is to be varied. These beneficiaries must be aged at least 18 and of sound mind. If one or more of the beneficiaries is a child (or an unborn member of a class of beneficiaries), it may still be possible to vary the will but the consent of a court will be required.

A variation cannot be revoked or changed again. But you could vary a will more than once if each variation dealt with different assets under the will.

Tax and variations

Provided certain conditions are met, the variation is treated for IHT and CGT purposes as if the new pattern of

Case Study Fred

When Fred died, his will revealed that he had left £600,000 to his wife, Betty, and the residue of his estate to his daughter, Linda. His daughter's share was £50,000 on which no tax was due, because Fred's taxable estate plus a couple of PETs made in the last seven years came to a running total of only £60,000.

Betty intends, when she dies, to leave everything to Linda, but this will mean a large IHT bill on an estate made up of Betty's own £20,000 and the £600,000 left to her by Fred. Assuming she had made no taxable gifts in the seven years before death, tax of 40% x [£620,000 – £300,000] = £128,000 would be payable (based on 2007-8 rates). But this bill could be reduced if some changes are made to Fred's will.

Betty does not need the whole £600,000, so she and Linda make a deed of variation directing that Fred's estate of £650,000 be split as follows: £290,000 to Linda – which, with the earlier PETs, uses up the whole of Fred's tax-free limit – and the residue of £310,000 to his wife.

There is still no IHT to pay on Fred's estate and the potential bill when Betty dies is reduced to [£310,000 + £20,000 – £300,000] x 40% = £12,000. This is a saving of £116,000.

bequests had been made by the deceased person. This means there are no IHT or CGT implications for you, but there could be IHT implications for the estate (and this might be a reason for making the variation). The conditions are:

- The variation is made within two years of the death.
- It is in writing, including specific wording to state that the variation is to be effective for IHT and CGT.
- You do not receive anything in return for making the variation, and
- If extra tax is due, the personal representatives must send a copy of the variation to HM Revenue & Customs.

A variation that does not meet the conditions would result in the new 'bequests' being treated as lifetime gifts (usually PETs) from the original beneficiaries to the new ones with the normal IHT and CGT (see Chapter 2) implications.

❝ Provided certain conditions are met, the variation is treated for IHT and CGT purposes as if the new pattern of bequests had been made by the deceased. ❞

201

Indexation factors and Retail Prices Index

Indexation factors for gifts you make from April 1998 onwards

Look along the left-hand or right-hand side to find the year in which you acquired the asset or incurred the expense; run your eye across to the column for the relevant month. This is the indexation factor you should use (see page 41 for further information).

	Jan	Feb	Mar	Apr	May	Jun
1982	–	–	1.047	1.006	0.992	0.987
1983	0.968	0.960	0.956	0.929	0.921	0.917
1984	0.872	0.865	0.859	0.834	0.828	0.823
1985	0.783	0.769	0.752	0.716	0.708	0.704
1986	0.689	0.683	0.681	0.665	0.662	0.663
1987	0.626	0.620	0.616	0.597	0.596	0.596
1988	0.574	0.568	0.562	0.537	0.531	0.525
1989	0.465	0.454	0.448	0.423	0.414	0.409
1990	0.361	0.353	0.339	0.300	0.288	0.283
1991	0.249	0.242	0.237	0.222	0.218	0.213
1992	0.199	0.193	0.189	0.171	0.167	0.167
1993	0.179	0.171	0.167	0.156	0.152	0.153
1994	0.151	0.144	0.141	0.128	0.124	0.124
1995	0.114	0.107	0.102	0.091	0.087	0.085
1996	0.083	0.078	0.073	0.066	0.063	0.063
1997	0.053	0.049	0.046	0.040	0.036	0.032
1998	0.091	0.014	0.011	–	–	–

" Indexation allowance is the relevant initial value or allowable expense multiplied by the appropriate indexation factor. "

Jul	Aug	Sep	Oct	Nov	Dec	
0.986	0.985	0.987	0.977	0.967	0.971	1982
0.906	0.898	0.889	0.883	0.876	0.871	1983
0.825	0.808	0.804	0.793	0.788	0.789	1984
0.707	0.703	0.704	0.701	0.695	0.693	1985
0.667	0.662	0.654	0.652	0.638	0.632	1986
0.597	0.593	0.588	0.580	0.573	0.574	1987
0.524	0.507	0.500	0.485	0.478	0.474	1988
0.408	0.404	0.395	0.384	0.372	0.369	1989
0.282	0.269	0.258	0.248	0.251	0.252	1990
0.215	0.213	0.208	0.204	0.199	0.198	1991
0.171	0.171	0.166	0.162	0.164	0.168	1992
0.156	0.151	0.146	0.147	0.148	0.146	1993
0.129	0.124	0.121	0.120	0.119	0.114	1994
0.091	0.085	0.080	0.085	0.085	0.079	1995
0.067	0.062	0.057	0.057	0.057	0.053	1996
0.032	0.026	0.021	0.019	0.019	0.016	1997
-	-	-	-	-	-	1998

Retail Prices Index (RPI). Base: January 1987 = 100

Use this chart if you need to work out the indexation factor for a period ending before April 1998 (see page 41 for further information).

	Jan	Feb	Mar	Apr	May	Jun
1982	–	–	79.44	81.04	81.62	81.85
1983	82.61	82.97	83.12	84.28	84.64	84.84
1984	86.84	87.20	87.48	88.64	88.97	89.20
1985	91.20	91.94	92.80	94.78	95.21	95.41
1986	96.25	96.60	96.73	97.67	97.85	97.79
1987	100.0	100.4	100.6	101.8	101.9	101.9
1988	103.3	103.7	104.1	105.8	106.2	106.6
1989	111.0	111.8	112.3	114.3	115.0	115.4
1990	119.5	120.2	121.4	125.1	126.2	126.7
1991	130.2	130.9	131.4	133.1	133.5	134.1
1992	135.6	136.3	136.7	138.8	139.3	139.3
1993	137.9	138.8	139.3	140.6	141.1	141.0
1994	141.3	142.1	142.5	144.2	144.7	144.7
1995	146.0	146.9	147.5	149.0	149.6	149.8
1996	150.2	150.9	151.5	152.6	152.9	153.0
1997	154.4	155.0	155.4	156.3	156.9	157.5
1998	159.5	160.3	160.8	162.6	–	–

Jul	Aug	Sep	Oct	Nov	Dec	
81.88	81.90	81.85	82.26	82.66	82.51	1982
85.30	85.68	86.06	86.36	86.67	86.89	1983
89.10	89.94	90.11	90.67	90.95	90.87	1984
95.23	95.49	95.44	95.59	95.92	96.05	1985
97.52	97.82	98.30	98.45	99.29	99.62	1986
101.8	102.1	102.4	102.9	103.4	103.3	1987
106.7	107.9	108.4	109.5	110.0	110.3	1988
115.5	115.8	116.6	117.5	118.5	118.8	1989
126.8	128.1	129.3	130.3	130.0	129.9	1990
133.8	134.1	134.6	135.1	135.6	135.7	1991
138.8	138.9	139.4	139.9	139.7	139.2	1992
140.7	141.3	141.9	141.8	141.6	141.9	1993
144.0	144.7	145.0	145.2	145.3	146.0	1994
149.1	149.9	150.6	149.8	149.8	150.7	1995
152.4	153.1	153.8	153.8	153.9	154.4	1996
157.5	158.5	159.3	159.5	159.6	160.0	1997
-	-	-	-	-	-	1998

Indexation factors and Retail Prices Index

Glossary

Administrators: The name given to your personal representatives if you have not made a will. They will distribute your estate in accordance with the law.

Alternative Investment Market (AIM): A junior section of the London Stock Exchange designed for companies that do not qualify for the main market, for example, because they are too small or do not have a long enough track record. Generally, AIM companies tend to be relatively new, small and/or growing so tend to be high-risk investments.

Arm's length: The term HM Revenue & Customs use to describe the sort of commercial transaction you would make with someone you did not know on the open market as opposed to a special arrangement you might strike with a friend or family member.

Asset: Anything you own, for example, cash, investments, a house, your personal possessions or anything else. Something you owe to someone else – such as an outstanding mortgage loan – is called a 'liability'.

Bare trust: Arrangement where someone holds as nominee for another person who, for tax purposes, is treated as if they own the assets outright.

Beneficiary: A person (or organisation) who may receive property from a trust or who has been left something in a will.

Bereaved minor's trust: A trust set up in the will of a parent who has died to benefit their child(ren). Provided certain conditions are met, special IHT rules apply instead of the normal rules that apply to most trusts from 22 March 2006 onwards.

Capital gains tax (CGT): Tax on the gain you make from selling an asset for more than it was worth when you started to own it. If you give the asset away, you are deemed to have made a gain if the asset has risen in value during the time you owned it. In practice, there may be no CGT to pay because you can deduct various reliefs and allowances.

Chattels: A tax term for those of your possessions tht are physical and portable, such as cars, jewellery, furniture, antiques, paintings, and so on.

Capital risk: The risk of losing some or all of the money you invest because the value of the investment can fall as well as rise.

Disabled person's trust: A trust set up either in life or in a will for the benefit of someone with a disability. Provided certain conditions are met, special IHT rules apply instead of the normal rules

206

that apply to most trusts from 22 March 2006 onwards.

Discretionary trust: A trust set up either in life or in a will where none of the beneficiaries has an interest in possession (see below) and the distribution of the trust assets and any income from them is at the discretion of the trustees.

Disposal: In the context of CGT, ceasing to own an asset, for example, because you sell it or give it away.

Domicile: Broadly the place where you make your permanent home and intend to end your days. However, for the purposes of IHT, you are treated as still UK-domiciled during the first three years after you have acquired a domicile in another country, or if you have been a UK resident for 17 of the last 20 tax years.

Estate: Everything you own at the time you die less everything you owe. For example, your estate includes your home, your furniture, car, personal possessions, savings and investments less your mortgage, tax you owe, unpaid bills, and so on. If you own something jointly with someone else (or have a joint mortgage or other debts), your estate includes just your share.

Executors: The name given to your personal representatives if you have made a will. They will try to ensure that the instructions in your will are carried out.

Gift aid: A scheme with tax incentives to encourage people to give to charity.

Gift with reservation: This occurs when you give something away but carry on using or enjoying it. For IHT purposes, you are treated as if you still own the asset.

Gross gift: A gift where the person receiving the gift pays any tax due.

Grossed-up amount: An amount you receive with tax already deducted plus either the tax deducted or the tax credit received with the amount.

Immediate post-death interest trust: A trust set up in a will that meets certain conditions and which gives someone – for example, your spouse or civil partner – the right to income from, or use of, the assets held by the trust. Provided all the conditions are met, special IHT rules apply instead of the normal rules that apply to most trusts from 22 March 2006 onwards.

Indexation allowance: An allowance you can claim that gives you relief from CGT on gains that are deemed to be just the result of inflation since March 1982 or the date you started to own the asset, whichever is later, up to April 1998.

Inheritance tax (IHT): Tax that may be due on some gifts you make in your lifetime and on your estate when you die. Tax is worked out by looking at the running total of taxable gifts in the seven years up to making the lifetime gift or death. If the total comes to more than your IHT-free limit, tax is due.

Interest in possession: The right to receive income from, or to use, assets held by a trust.

Interest-in-possession trust: A trust set up in life or in a will where one or

207

more of the beneficiaries has the right to receive income from, or to use, assets held by the trust.

Intestacy: Dying without having made a will. The law sets out how your estate will be distributed.

Joint tenancy: A way of sharing the ownership of an asset. All the owners had equal shares and identical rights to enjoy the whole asset. On the death of an owner, their share automatically passes to the surviving owner(s).

Net gift: A gift where the person making the gift pays any tax due. The tax paid counts as part of the gift.

Nil-rate band: Another name for the IHT-free limit.

Non-resident and not ordinarily resident: This is likely to apply if you go to work full-time abroad and the following conditions are met: your absence from the UK and your contract of employment both last at least a whole tax year; your visits back to the UK add up to less than 183 days in any one tax year; and your visits back to the UK average 91 days per tax year or less. By concession, a husband, wife or civil partner accompanying their spouse to work abroad can also count as non-resident. If you go abroad for reasons other than work – say, you retire abroad – to count as non-resident, you will need to convince HM Revenue & Customs that you have severed your ties with the UK.

Ordinarily resident: This normally applies if you live in the UK year after year, even if you are away temporarily.

Payroll giving: A scheme with tax incentives to encourage employees to give to charity.

Personal representative: The person, people or organisation that sees that your estate is distributed following your death.

Potentially exempt transfer (PET): A lifetime gift between individuals (or occasionally a trust). There is no IHT on the gift provided the giver survives seven years. If they don't, the gift is reassessed as a taxable gifts and IHT on it may become due after all.

Pre-owned assets tax (POAT): Income tax on any benefit you are deemed still to get from an asset you once used to own or have contributed towards the purchase of. But, if the gift is caught by the gift-with-reservation rules (see above), their will be no POAT to pay.

Resident: You will always count as resident in the UK if you spend 183 days or more of the tax year in the UK. You may still count as resident even if you spend fewer days here.

Residue: Whatever remains of your estate after all your debts, expenses and specific legacies and gifts have been made.

Reversionary interest: The right to receive assets from a trust at some specified time or when some specified event occurs. In the meantime, you have no right to the assets or income from them or use of them.

Settlement: A term that is used in tax legislation to mean most arrangements or agreements that transfers assets with some element of 'bounty' (meaning some element of gift to the recipient). Trusts are sometimes referred to as settlements but 'settlement' includes many other types of arrangement as well.

Tenancy in common: A way of sharing ownership of an asset. The owners have specified shares which may be unequal and which they can sell or give away without the consent of the other owners. On death, an owner's share is passed on according to their will or the intestacy rules.

Taper relief: In the context of CGT, a reduction in the value of a gain on which tax may be due. The reduction increases according to the number of years the asset has been owned. In the context of IHT, a reduction in any tax due on a PET, which has become taxable because the giver died within seven years of making the gift.

Testator/testatrix: The man or woman whose will it is. You must be aged 18 or over (and of sound mind) to make a valid will.

Trust: A legal arrangement where one or more people (the trustees) hold money or assets (the trust property) to be used for the benefit of one or more other people (the beneficiaries). The trust's rules can set conditions on how the trust property is held and used.

Variation: The process of changing the gifts made under a will after the person who made the will has died.

Useful addresses

Accountant – to find one

Association of Chartered Certified
Accountants
29 Lincoln's Inn Fields
London WC2A 3EE
Tel: 020 7396 7000.
www.acca.co.uk

Institute of Chartered Accountants in
England and Wales
PO Box 433
Chartered Accountants' Hall
Moorgate Place
London EC2P 2BJ
Tel: 020 7920 8100
www.icaew.co.uk

Institute of Chartered Accountants in
Ireland
CA House
83 Pembroke Road
Dublin 4
Republic of Ireland
Tel: (00 353) 1 637 7200
www.icai.ie

Institute of Chartered Accountants of
Scotland
CA House
21 Haymarket Yards
Edinburgh EH12 5BH
Tel: 0131 347 0100
www.icas.org.uk

Charities Aid Foundation

25 Kings Hill Avenue
Kings Hill
West Malling
Kent ME19 4TA
Tel: 01732 520000
www.cafonline.org.uk
CAF Charity Account:
www.allaboutgiving.org

Charity Commission

London
Harmsworth House
13–15 Bouverie Street
London EC4Y 8DP
(Central Register open 9am–5pm)

Liverpool
12 Princes Dock
Princes Parade
Liverpool L3 1DE
(Central register open 9am–4.30pm)

Newport
8th Floor, Clarence House
Clarence Place
Newport NP19 7AA

Taunton
Woodfield House
Tangier
Taunton
Somerset TA1 4BL
(Central Register open 9.30am–4pm)
Tel: 0845 3000218
www.charitycommission.gov.uk

Discount broker – some examples

www.chasedevere.co.uk
www.h-l.co.uk

Financial Ombudsman Service

South Quay Plaza
183 Marsh Wall
London E14 9SR
Tel: 0845 080 1800
Website: www. financial_ombudsman.org.uk

Fund supermarket – some examples

www.adviceonline.co.uk/
investdecisiontree.html
www.fidelity.co.uk
(Funds Network)
www.h-l.co.uk
www.tqonline.co.uk

HM Revenue & Customs (HMRC)

- For local tax enquiry centres look in The Phone Book under 'HM Revenue & Customs'.
- For your local tax office, check your tax return, other tax correspondence or check with your employer
- See also Capital Taxes Office above
- HMRC Orderline (IHT): 0845 234 1000
- HMRC Orderline (self-assessment): 0845 9000 404
- HMRC Orderline (taxback for non-taxpayers): 0845 9000 444
- Website: www.hmrc.gov.uk
- Child trust fund website: www.childtrustfund.gov.uk

HMRC Inheritance Tax

(HM Revenue & Customs)

England and Wales
Ferrers House
Castle Meadow Road
Nottingham NG2 1BB

Northern Ireland
Level 3
Dorchester House
52–58 Great Victoria Street
Belfast BT2 7QL

Scotland
Meldrum House
15 Drumsheugh Gardens
Edinburgh EH3 7UG

Tel: 0845 234 1000 (for forms and leaflets)

IHT200 Orderline: 0845 234 1020
Probate & IHT Helpline: 0845 30 20 900
www.hmrc.gov.uk/cto

Independent Financial Adviser – to find one

IFA Promotion
For a list of IFAs in your area, contact the telephone number below.
Tel: 0800 085 3250
www.unbiased.co.uk

The Institute of Financial Planning
Whitefriars Centre
Lewins Mead
Bristol BS1 2NT
Tel: 0117 9345 2470
www.financialplanning.org.uk

MyLocalAdviser
www.mylocaladviser.co.uk

211

Personal Finance Society (PFS)
For a list of IFAs who have more than just
the basic qualifications, contact:
20 Aldermanbury
London EC2V 7HY
Tel: 020 8530 0852
www.thepfs.org

Institute of Professional Will Writers

Trinity Point
New Road, Halesowen
West Midlands B63 3HY
Tel: 08456 44 20 42
www.ipw.org.uk

Insurance broker – to find one

British Insurance Brokers Association (BIBA)
For a list of brokers in your area, contact
BIBA at:
14 Bevis Marks
London EC3A 7NT
Tel: 0870 950 1790
www.biba.org.uk

MyLocalAdviser
www.mylocaladviser.co.uk

Law Societies

The Law Society (England and Wales)
113 Chancery Lane
London WC2A 1PL
Tel: 0870 606 6575
www.lawsociety.co.uk

The Law Society of Northern Ireland
Law Society House
98 Victoria Street
Belfast BT1 3JZ
Tel: 028 90 2316 14
www.lawsoc-ni.org

The Law Society of Scotland
26 Drumsheugh Gardens
Edinburgh EH3 7YR
Tel: 0131 226 7411
Client Relations Office (complaints): 0845
113 0018
www.lawscot.org.uk

Law Society Consumer Complaints
Service (England & Wales)
Victoria Court
8 Dormer Place
Leamington Spa
Warwickshire CV32 5AE
Helpline: 0845 608 6565
Minicom: 0845 601 1682
www.lawsociety.org.uk

National Council for Voluntary Organisations (NCVO)

Regent's Wharf
8 All Saints Street
London N1 9RL
Tel: 0800 2798 798
www.ncvo-vol.org.uk

National Savings & Investments (NS&I)

Children's bonus bonds, investment
account
Glasgow G58 1SB

Premium Bonds
Blackpool FY3 9YP

Cash mini ISA
Durham DH99 1NS

Tel: 0845 964 5000
www.nsandi.com

212

Office of the Scottish Charity Regulator

2nd Floor, Quadrant House
9 Riverside Drive
Dundee DD1 4NY
Tel: 01382 220446
www.oscr.org.uk

Probate Registry (England & Wales)

To obtain probate forms, leaflets and information
- Your local Probate Registry. See Phone Book under 'Probate Registry'
- Probate & IHT Helpline: 0845 30 20 900
- www.hmcourts-service.gov.uk/cms/wills.htm

Probate and Matrimonial Office (Northern Ireland)

Royal Courts of Justice (Northern Ireland)
Chichester Street
Belfast BT1 3JF
Tel: 028 9023 5111
www.courtsni.gov.uk

Sheriff's Court (Scotland)

To obtain confirmation forms, leaflets and information
- Your local Sheriff Clerk. See Phone Book under 'Sheriff's Court'
- Operations & Policy Unit, Scottish Court Service Headquarters, Hayweight House, 23 Lauriston Street, Edinburgh EH3 9DQ Tel: 0131 229 9200
- www.scotcourts.gov.uk/sheriff/index.asp

Society of Will Writers

Eagle House, Exchange Road
Lincoln LN6 3JZ
Tel: 01522 687888
www.thesocietyofwillwriters.co.uk

Solicitor – to find one

Contact the Law Societies above or Society of Trust and Estate Practitioners below

Society of Trust and Estate Practitioners (STEP)

26 Grosvenor Gardems
London SW1W OGT
Tel: 020 7838 4890
www.step.org

Stockbroker – to find one

Association of Private Client Investment Managers and Stockbrokers (APCIMS)
114 Middlesex Street
London E1 7JH
Tel: 020 7247 7080
www.apcims.co.uk

London Stock Exchange
10 Paternoster Square
London EC4M 7LS
Tel: 020 7797 1000
www.londonstockexchange.com

Tax adviser – to find one

The Chartered Institute of Taxation
12 Upper Belgrave Street
London SW1X 8BB
Tel: 020 7235 9381
www.tax.org.uk

Will Aid

The next Will Aid campaign takes place in November 2008
Tel: 0870 6060 239
www.willaid.org.uk

Useful addresses

213

Index

Index

215

Index

Index

Index

which?

Which? Books

Other books in this series

The Tax Handbook 2007/8
By Tony Levene
ISBN: 978 1 84490 039 8
Price £10.99

Make sense of the complicated rules, legislation and red-tape with the *Tax Handbook 2007/8*. Written by Guardian finance journalist and tax expert Tony Levene, this essential guide gives expert advice on all aspects of the UK tax system and does the footwork for you. It includes information on finding the right accountant and how to get the best from them, advice on NI contributions, tax credits for families and the self-assessment form. An indispensable guide for anyone who pays tax.

The Pension Handbook
By Jonquil Lowe
ISBN: 978 1 84490 025 1
Price £10.99

A definitive guide to sorting out your pension, whether you're deliberating over SERPs/S2Ps, organising a personal pension or moving schemes. Cutting through confusion and dispelling apathy, Jonquil Lowe provides up-to-date advice on how to maximise your savings and provide for the future.

Buy, Sell and Move House
By Kate Faulkner
ISBN: 978 1 84490 030 5
Price £10.99

A complete, no-nonsense guide to negotiating the property maze and making your move as painless as possible. From dealing with estate agents to chasing solicitors, working out the true cost of your move to understanding Home Information Packs, this guide tells you how to keep things on track and avoid painful sticking points.

which?

Which? Books

Other books in this series

What To Do When Someone Dies
By Paul Harris
ISBN: 978 1 84490 028 2
Price £10.99

Coping with bereavement is never easy but this book makes dealing with the formalities as straightforward and simple as possible. Covering all the practicalities, this book provides step-by-step guidance on registering a death, making funeral arrangements, applying for probate and sorting out the financial matters.

Wills and Probate
By Paul Elmhirst
ISBN: 978 1 84490 033 6
Price £10.99

Wills and Probate provides clear, easy-to-follow guidance on the main provisions to make in a will and the factors you should consider when drafting these. The second part of the book provides step-by-step guidance on probate, making the process as straightforward and trouble-free as possible. By being aware of key changes and revisions and avoiding the problems and pitfalls, you can limit delays, avoid disputes and save tax.

Divorce and Splitting Up
By Imogen Clout
ISBN: 978 1 84490 034 3
Price £10.99

Divorce, separation, dissolution of a civil partnership or simply splitting up with a partner is never easy – the emotional upheaval, legal complexities and financial implications make even the most amicable parting a demanding business; when children are involved, couples are in dispute and property needs to be divided the whole process can be fraught with difficulties. *Divorce and Splitting Up* offers comprehensive, clear, step-by-step guidance through the whole process, explaining how the law works, drawing attention to key considerations and looking at ways of minimising unnecessary conflict and costs.

Which? Books

Which? Books provide impartial, expert advice on everyday matters from finance to law, property to major life events. We also publish the country's most trusted restaurant guide, *The Which? Good Food Guide*. To find out more about Which? Books, log on to www.which.co.uk or call 01903 828557.

"Which? tackles the issues that really matter to consumers and gives you the advice and active support you need to buy the right products."